Python Made Easy

Marco Gähler

Python Made Easy

A Beginner's Guide to Coding, Data Structures, and Practical Applications

Apress®

Marco Gähler
Zürich, Zürich, Switzerland

ISBN 979-8-8688-2132-5   ISBN 979-8-8688-2133-2   (eBook)
https://doi.org/10.1007/979-8-8688-2133-2

© Marco Gähler 2026

This work is subject to copyright. All rights are solely and exclusively licensed by the Publisher, whether the whole or part of the material is concerned, specifically the rights of translation, reprinting, reuse of illustrations, recitation, broadcasting, reproduction on microfilms or in any other physical way, and transmission or information storage and retrieval, electronic adaptation, computer software, or by similar or dissimilar methodology now known or hereafter developed.
The use of general descriptive names, registered names, trademarks, service marks, etc. in this publication does not imply, even in the absence of a specific statement, that such names are exempt from the relevant protective laws and regulations and therefore free for general use.
The publisher, the authors and the editors are safe to assume that the advice and information in this book are believed to be true and accurate at the date of publication. Neither the publisher nor the authors or the editors give a warranty, expressed or implied, with respect to the material contained herein or for any errors or omissions that may have been made. The publisher remains neutral with regard to jurisdictional claims in published maps and institutional affiliations.

This Apress imprint is published by the registered company APress Media, LLC, part of Springer Nature.
The registered company address is: 1 New York Plaza, New York, NY 10004, U.S.A.

If disposing of this product, please recycle the paper.

Declarations

Competing Interests The author has no competing interests to declare that are relevant to the content of this manuscript.

Contents

1 About Python 1
    The REPL 1
    Advantages and Drawbacks of Python 3
    Importing Libraries 3
    Style Guides 4
        Software Engineering Made Easy 5
        The Zen of Python 5

2 Naming 7
    Naming Rules 9
    Naming Conventions 9
    Writing Readable Names 11

3 Components of Code 13
    Mutable and Immutable Objects 13
    Assignments 14
    Types 15
    Variables 15
        Global Variables 16
    None 17
    Numbers 17
        Floating Point Numbers 17
        Integers 18
        Strings and Numbers 19
    Booleans 19
    Lists 20
        Creating Lists 20
        Accessing Lists 22
        Accessing Sublists 24
        Multidimensional Lists 25
        Sorting lists 26
        Merging Lists 27
        How to Continue 27
    Strings 28
        Various Types of Strings 29
        String Operations 30
    Dicts 31
    Tuples 32

	Tuples vs. Lists	33
	Enums	34
	Rarely Used Data Structures	35
	Sets	35
	Exceptions	35
	Try, Catch, Else, Finally	36
	When to Use Exceptions	37
	Pitfalls	37
	Custom Exceptions	38
	Code Structure	39
	Coupling and Cohesion	40
4	**Loops and If Statements**	**43**
	Loops	43
	Nested Loops	44
	If Statements	44
	Nested If Statements	45
	Boolean Logic	46
	Return, Break, and Continue	47
	Return	47
	Break	47
	Continue	47
5	**Basic Mathematics**	**49**
	Basic Mathematics with Python	49
	Arithmetic Operations	49
	The Math Module	50
	NumPy	51
	Matrices	51
	Images	52
	Random Numbers	55
	Calculating Pi	56
6	**Functions and Methods**	**57**
	Keyword Arguments	58
	Default Arguments	59
	args and kwargs	60
	Function Overloading	61
	Control Flow	62
	Function Definition Order	62
	Cyclic Dependencies	63
	Recursion	63
	Trees	64
7	**Classes**	**67**
	Classes and Objects	69
	Special Methods	70
	Example	71
	Inheritance	75
	Implementation Inheritance	75

		Interface Inheritance	77
	Encapsulation		78
	Abstraction		79
8	**Python Modules and Packages**		81
	Modules and Imports		81
		Regular Packages	81
		Namespace Packages	82
	Installing Packages with Pip		83
	The Virtual Environment		84
9	**Util**		85
	Files		85
		CSV	85
		JSON and Co	86
		HDF5	87
		SQL	87
		Summary	88
	Time		89
		Timing Functions	89
10	**Unit Tests**		91
	Why Tests?		91
	How to Write Tests		92
		What to Test	94
	Test-Driven Development		94
		Example of TDD	95
	Dependency Injection		97
		Mocking	101
		Faking	101
11	**Matplotlib**		103
	Simple Plots		103
	Labeling		105
	Histograms		105
	Curve Fitting		106
		Local Minima of Curve Fitting	108
12	**Pandas**		109
	Pandas Example		109
13	**Numerical Mathematics**		115
	Numerical Integration		116
		Mathematical Derivation	116
		Geometric Interpretation	117
		Higher Order Integration	118
		Estimating the Accuracy	119
		Monte Carlo Integration	119

  Numerical Solution of Differential Equations 120
    Differential Equations 120
    Coupled Differential Equations 122

14 Some Examples 125
  Percolation 125

Index 131

About the Author

Marco Gähler began his career studying physics at ETH Zurich before transitioning to software engineering. In 2018, he joined Zurich Instruments, where he developed electronic devices used in quantum computing. At the time of writing, he is founding a company EasyCare, which organizes home treatment of elderly people.

Throughout his career, Marco has observed the pitfalls in code written by self-taught developers, for example, PhD students, and recognized the need for clear, practical guidance on simple programming practices.

About the Technical Reviewer

Shibsankar Das is currently working as a senior data scientist at Microsoft. He has 10+ years of experience working in IT where he has led several data science initiatives, and in 2019, he was recognized as one of the top 40 data scientists in India. His core strength is in GenAI, deep learning, NLP, and graph neural networks. Currently, he is focusing on his research on AI agents and knowledge graphs. He has experience working in the domain of foundational research, FinTech, and ecommerce.

Before Microsoft, he worked at Optum, Walmart, Envestnet, Microsoft Research, and Capgemini. He pursued a master's from the Indian Institute of Technology, Bangalore.

Introduction

Is there a reason to write a book about programming in times of artificial intelligence (AI)? I think, yes, there is. You still have to learn the fundamentals of programming, and that's what this book is about. AI can do many things by now, but it cannot replace yet every part of software engineering. And this is where this book comes into place. I try to give you an idea of what programming is about, about the pitfalls of Python, and what Python has to offer.

I didn't write exercises in this book because I think the best way of learning a programming language is by doing a project. I never really solved the exercises anyway; learning by doing is, in my opinion, the much more effective way of learning.

This book is not going to teach you everything there is to know about Python. It's simply impossible to learn too many things. Though there are books on Python that tried, these are 1000 pages long and feel more like encyclopedias. I didn't want to write such a book because who reads 1000 pages about Python? I think it's much more efficient to write a concise book that you can read back to back and later on you will anyway use Google or an AI assistant to find the information you need. I think a book on a programming language should give you an idea of how the programming language works and what it can do. It should only kick start your journey into this new language. The times of printed encyclopedias are over.

I wrote this book with scientists and engineers in mind. Of course, you can also do web development, IT security, and many other things with Python. But I didn't write about these things. Explaining the Django web framework or some IT security is too specific for this book and out of scope. Science and engineering, on the other hand, need very little knowledge in order to get started. Furthermore, scientists and engineers have the potential to become good programmers. But first, they have to learn it properly, which, unfortunately, is something many experienced programmers didn't do. And for this reason, there is a lot of bad code out there.

When programming, you often have to find out why something doesn't work as it should, so you have to follow the traces of the code to find the error. You also have to structure the knowledge you have about the code as well as possible and thus make it available to your coworkers. Knowing how to work scientifically is a great advantage in programming.

This book is only the beginning. It takes some intrinsic motivation to become a good programmer. For this reason, there are no exercises in this book, nor is it hundreds of pages long explaining all kinds of things you won't remember. Instead, I tried to write a concise book that you can really read back to back. Though I have to admit that I also added some examples of mathematical problems for scientists and engineers toward the end of the book for the interested reader. But you don't have to read them if you're not interested in them.

Usually by far the best way of learning programming is having a personal project to work on. This gives you a goal and practical experience. You also learn to work independently. This book won't teach you everything that you need to know for your project; it is only able to give you a jump start. You can take some of the things that you learned and combine them into something new. But you also have to find out a lot of things yourself. Here, your best friend is good old Google, or also some of the many AI tools that can answer your questions as well.

Once you get started, it is important to keep learning. Ask some friends for advice to improve your code, do an internship, watch YouTube videos, or read books that help you write better code. For example, my other book, *Software Engineering Made Easy*, further explains many of the gray boxes you will find in this book. Learn from different sources and compare their advice. Programming is not an exact science, and you will have to find out what works best for you. There's an infinite number of ways to solve a problem, and you have to find the one that works best for you.

About Python

Python is a universal, interpreted, high-level programming language. It was developed in 1991 by Guido van Rossum and is named after the comedy group Monty Python. The current version, 3, was released in 2008, with new features being added all the time. Python is so widely used that it is preinstalled on most operating systems. Simply search your operating system for "Python," or open the command line and type. If, contrary to expectations, it is not installed, you can download and install Python from python.org.

Python is an interpreted language; it executes code line by line, which enhances flexibility and speeds up development. This feature makes it ideal for beginners and professionals alike, allowing real-time feedback and simplifying the debugging process. Its interpreted nature also supports dynamic typing and interactive execution, making Python a preferred choice for rapid prototyping, scripting, and automation across platforms.

The REPL

Since Python is an interpreted language (the alternative would be a compiled language), there is also a special command line that allows you to run Python code. This is also called a "REPL" (Read-Eval-Print Loop). You can also tell whether some code examples are executed in the REPL by the fact that every line with user input begins with > > > or . . . .

In Figure 1.1 you can see a screenshot of the REPL, which I opened in PowerShell by typing `Python`.

The alternative is to write code in a text editor (without formatting, not Word!) and then save it as a .py file, for example, PrintAddress.py. You can then run this code in the normal command line by calling Python with `python PrintAddress.py` and the entire code will be executed. If you write code that is longer than just a few lines, I recommend that you save it in a special text file and not use the REPL.

At the time of writing, I use the VS Code integrated development environment (IDE) for writing code. I recommend you use it as well, unless you have a friend helping you with another IDE.

> **Using the REPL**
> The REPL is great for playing around with a few lines of code, but for longer code, it becomes tedious to use. I use it only for short code snippets.

© The Author(s), under exclusive license to APress Media, LLC, part of Springer Nature 2026
M. Gähler, *Python Made Easy*,
https://doi.org/10.1007/979-8-8688-2133-2_1

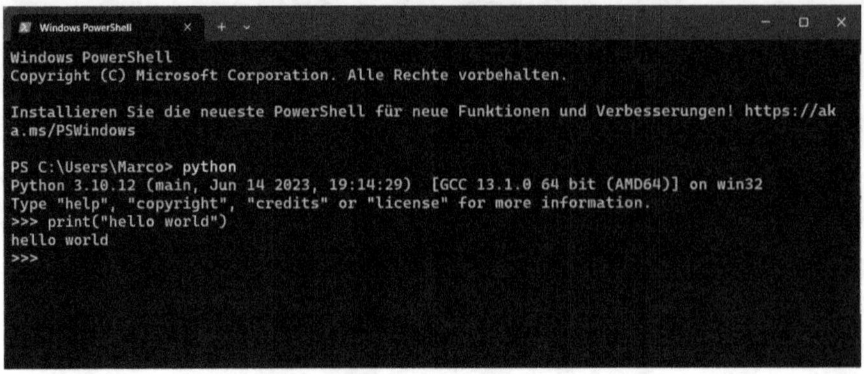

Fig. 1.1 The REPL of Python started in PowerShell. I have already executed the "hello world" command on the last three lines

As far as I know, there is only one somewhat significant difference between the REPL and executing code as a text file. This is the way you can inspect an object. In "normal" code, you have to call the `print` function to do this.

Meanwhile, in the REPL, you can omit the `print` command and just enter the variable itself. The REPL then returns the value of the variable.

```
>>> "echo"
'echo'
```

In this short example, we also saw the syntactical difference between the REPL and the code in text form. In the REPL, we write a >>> before each new line. You don't have to enter this yourself; that would be very tedious and pointless. Instead, this is simply the way to show that you are in the REPL and not, for example, in the normal command line or in the text editor.

Whether you use the REPL or prefer to write code as normal text is largely up to you. As I wrote before, I recommend that you write longer pieces of code as text and only use the REPL when you want to inspect the effect of one or two lines of code. Writing long pieces of code in the REPL is possible but tedious.

An alternative to the REPL is the Jupyter Notebook. Jupyter allows you to execute code in your browser and display the results directly. Jupyter is useful for small- to intermediate-sized projects, such as some data analysis. For larger projects, I recommend using pure code files, as this allows you to use version control systems like Git.

> **Git**
> Git is *the* version control system. Most professional software companies use it. With Git, you can take snapshots of your code and jump back and forth between them. Furthermore, there are websites like GitHub that host Git projects, making it easy to back up your code. Git is also great for collaborating with others. You should learn Git as soon as you start your first bigger project.

Advantages and Drawbacks of Python

While Python is great for faster development due to the fact that it is an interpreted language without the need for defining types, it has its drawbacks when writing large-scale software. The types of variables and arguments are not just boilerplate code; they are an important piece of information. For this reason, Python also introduced type hints, even though they are neither mandatory nor enforced. You could take the following function add and pass it two strings instead of ints.

```
def add(a: int, b: int) -> int:
    return a + b

add("hello ", "world") # returns "hello world"
```

A compiler can give you a lot of important information when writing code. It's an advantage that you save some time as you don't have to wait for the compiler after every change you make, but on the other hand, running the unit tests in Python may take some time, as executing code in Python is slow. In bigger projects, this may outweigh the time you save by not having to compile the code. These are drawbacks to consider when starting a new project and considering using Python as your programming language.

Though there are tools like pylint that can give you some warnings if your code is off, they do not replace the capabilities of a full-fledged compiler. The only other thing that can check your code for errors is unit tests (p. 91). For this reason, it is even more important to write unit tests in Python than in compiled languages.

Generally, I don't recommend using Python for larger projects. It is a great language for small- to medium-sized projects, but if you are working on a large project, I recommend using a compiled language like Rust, Java, or C++. These languages are much more efficient with memory usage and much faster, and the compiler can give you a lot of useful information; meanwhile, in Python, you'll only find errors at runtime.

Importing Libraries

As in any commonly used programming language, there is a plethora of libraries available for Python.

Libraries are collections of prewritten code that provide functions and tools for specific tasks, such as data analysis, web development, or machine learning. They save time and effort by eliminating the need to write code from scratch, allowing developers to build applications more efficiently and with fewer errors. In Python, there are libraries for pretty much any programming topic that you could think of.

In order to use a third-party library, you first have to install it, unless it is one of the few standard libraries that are already preinstalled. Installing a library can be done in many different ways. The easiest one is using the `pip` command. Pip is the package manager for Python and is installed by default when you install Python. You have to open the command line and run `pip install numpy` to install the NumPy library, for example.

> **Virtual Environments**
>
> While it is possible to call `pip install numpy` in the command line, it is generally recommended to use a virtual environment because different projects that you work on may have different dependencies. Furthermore, there are plenty of tools that simplify the management of dependencies using virtual environments.
>
> Here is a short example of how to create a virtual environment and install NumPy in it. Note that there is a minor difference between Linux and Windows. On Linux, you have to use `source venv/bin/activate` to activate the virtual environment, while on Windows, you have to use `venv\Scripts\activate`.
>
> ```
> python -m venv venv
> source venv/bin/activate
> pip install numpy
> ```
>
> If you are working on a serious project, you will be collaborating with other developers. Then it's worth creating a `requirements.txt` file that lists all the dependencies of your project. This file can be used to install all dependencies with a single command. You can install libraries with the following command:
>
> ```
> pip install -r requirements.txt
> ```

In order to use a library in your project, you have to import it. In Python, this is fairly simple. You just write `import numpy` at the beginning of your code.

Style Guides

Software development is not an exact science where there is only right or wrong. Instead, there are endless ways to implement a certain functionality. Some of them are better than others. There are websites, YouTube videos, and a plethora of books, including my own,[1] with tips on how to write good code. A few examples are the Zen of Python[2] or the Google Style Guide.[3] I can highly recommend reading through these resources as they help you get an idea of how to write good code.

> **Learning Programming**
>
> This book won't be sufficient to learn programming. It only serves as a short overview of what you *can* learn. The best way to learn programming is to have a project to work on or at least to attend a course where you get exercises to solve. This gives you a goal and practical experience. If you encounter a problem you haven't faced before, you have to search the internet or ask an AI tool for advice. This is what programming is really about.
>
> The simplest way to get started solving a problem is to take some example code that does something similar to what you want to do and modify it until it does exactly what you want. In fact, this is generally a very efficient way to learn something new, not only in programming.

---

[1] Software Engineering Made Easy, Marco Gähler.
[2] https://peps.python.org/pep-0020/
[3] https://google.github.io/styleguide/pyguide.html

Software Engineering Made Easy

In my book *Software Engineering Made Easy*, I came up with four fundamental principles that I think are very important to adhere to.

- Write code that is easy to understand.

    As we'll see on p. 8, you'll spend much more time reading code than writing it. For this reason, it is of utmost importance that you write code that is easy to understand.

- Write code that can have as few bugs as possible.

    Humans are fallible; we make mistakes. For this reason, one should make code as fail-safe as possible. Of course, you cannot prevent all bugs, but you should try to make it as hard as possible for bugs to occur.

- Constantly clean up your code.

    Over time, the entropy of your code increases and it will become a mess. Just like anything else in the universe, entropy always increases and you have to fight it. At home, it is called cleaning up; in software, it is called refactoring.

- Write code to create value for your customers.

    There are many software engineers who love to discuss about meaningless details for hours. Please don't do this. You will be paid by your customers, and they want to have new features, not to pay for meaningless details.

The Zen of Python

- Explicit is better than implicit.
- Simple is better than complex.
- Readability counts.

    Smart people often tend to write implicit code because it is more efficient and I have to admit that implicit code can be beautiful. However, implicit code is often hard to read and understand, and therefore, it is more error-prone. For the same reason, you should keep the code also as simple as possible.

- Flat is better than nested.

    This is a very important principle. Nested code is often hard to read and understand, and therefore, it is more error-prone. And if you don't believe me, just write some nested loops with if/else statements and try to understand what the code does. You will have a hard time.

- Special cases aren't special enough to break the rules.
- Although practicality beats purity.

Write the code such that there are hardly any special cases, such that there are hardly any if statements. Though you should not overdo it. It is not worth to write a hundred lines of code only to replace one if statement.

- In the face of ambiguity, refuse the temptation to guess.

Guessing is done way too often in software engineering. It is better to write a few lines of code that are not needed than to guess what the code does. And if you are guessing, you should at least write some unit tests.

- There should be one—and preferably only one—obvious way to do it.

It is better to write the code in a way that there is only one way to do it than to write the code in a way that there are multiple ways to do it. This is because there is always the risk that you will forget to update one of the ways, and then you will have a bug in your code.

- If the implementation is hard to explain, it's a bad idea.
- If the implementation is easy to explain, it may be a good idea.

Code should be easy to understand. In most cases, others will have to understand the code without any help. If you can't explain the code to someone else, it is a sign that the code is not good enough. And if you ever happen to read code that you don't understand, it is not your fault. It's the fault of the author of the code. They didn't manage to write the code in a way that is easy to understand.

Naming

2

Now it might be a little surprising to you that I start this book with the chapter on naming. You were probably expecting some code, but there is no denying that naming is one of the most important and difficult things in software development.

Every variable (p. 15), function (p. 57), or class (p. 67) has a name. This name is generally the only description of an object that you have when reading code. You read the name, and you are supposed to know what the object does. It's just the same when I hear my name being called, and I know that somebody wants to talk to me. If there is someone else with the same name around, it will cause a lot of confusion.

For these reasons, naming is a very important and also a very difficult part of software development. A good name can make the code more understandable, while a bad name can make the code incomprehensible. However, finding good names is one of the hardest things in software development because there is no algorithm that tells you how to name things. You have to rely on your intuition and experience.

Let's take a quick look at an example with bad names.

```
def a(b, c):
    pass
```

As we can see, poorly chosen names cause the code to become incomprehensible. What is this code all about? We have no idea. We'd have to read through the implementation of the function to find out what it does. But this is extremely time-consuming and error-prone. It is much better to choose a good name for the function to begin with.

> **The Importance of Naming**
> Naming is one of the hardest, yet also one of the most important things in software development. Only with good names can your code be understood. If you choose the names poorly, it's like reading a foreign language. You won't understand a thing.

A much better name for this function would be, for example, `make_appointment`. With a good name, we have a pretty good idea of what the function does. There is probably no need to read through the implementation. This is the power of a good name.

```
def make_appointment(date, duration):
    pass
```

Now, of course, a name is not able to tell you everything. Finding a good name is hard and depends on many factors. The most important aspect is the context in which the name is used. For example, it is a priori not possible to say which of the following names is better:

- `price_of_apple`
- `price`
- `p`

Which of these names you should use depends on the context in which the variable is used. The `price_of_apple` is generally a good name, as it is descriptive yet not too long.

If you are at a market stall with apples, the name `price` is probably sufficient. You know that you are talking about the price of the apple.

If you are iterating over a list of prices and you need a variable for a line or two, you can also just use `p` as a name. It is clear from the context what `p` means, and you don't have to write the whole name.

```
prices = [1.99, 2.50, 3.99]
for p in prices:
    print(p)
```

> **What Programming is Really About**
> You are probably eager to learn how to write code. But first, we have to talk about what programming is all about, and Figure 2.1 sums it up nicely. If you do more than just write a few throwaway scripts, you will spend most of your time reading and understanding code. Writing code takes only a small fraction of the time. For this reason, it is extremely important to write code that is easy to understand. And this is only possible with good names.

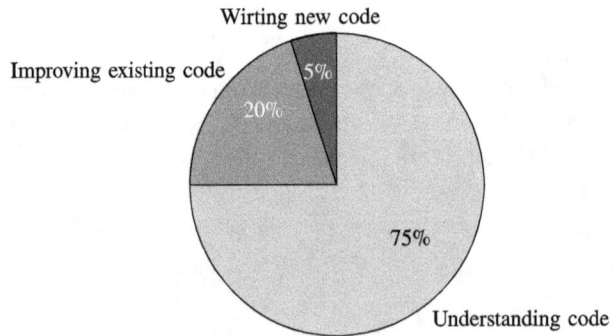

Fig. 2.1 Coding activities of a software engineer

> **Refactoring**
>
> Refactoring is the process of improving the structure of your code without changing its functionality. Refactoring is really important, as your code will otherwise become a Big Ball of Mud.[a] If you have enough tests in place (p. 91), refactoring can be really fun.
>
> ---
> [a] https://en.wikipedia.org/wiki/Anti-pattern#Big_ball_of_mud

Naming Rules

Names in Python should generally consist of letters and underscores. Though they should not start with a double underscore as these are reserved for special methods and could lead to a lot of confusion.

Furthermore, names may contain numbers, but not as the first character. However, I generally advice against using numbers in variable names. If you feel the urge to use a number in a variable name, it is usually a bad sign. The value of a variable should be a number, not its name.

In fact, one can use any Unicode character in a name that is not used for some sort of operation. Even emojis. But as cool as this sounds, I highly recommend against it. Not only are you running into potential compatibility issues with different editors, but you also make it harder for others to read your code. It is best to stick to letters and underscores.

When naming your variables, functions, and classes, you have almost complete freedom how you want to name them. The only exception are the keywords used by Python like `if`, `else`, `while`, `for`, `def`, `class`, etc. These keywords are reserved and cannot be used as names for variables, functions, or classes.

One thing you can do is overriding built-in functions. This is generally a bad idea, as it can lead to confusion and bugs in your code. For example, if you override the `print` function, you won't be able to print anything anymore. This is not only confusing for you but also for others who read your code.

Naming Conventions

Naming conventions are important to keep the code readable. As in all other programming languages, Python also has conventions for writing variables, functions, and classes. The common conventions for Python are recorded in.[1]

The names of functions and variables are written in lowercase in Python. If the name consists of several words, they are separated with an underscore. This is also known as "snake_case".

It is not possible to make a variable constant in Python. It is just a convention to write constants in uppercase letters. This is just a convention and not enforced by the interpreter. If you want to make a variable constant, you can write its name in uppercase letters, like `MY_CONSTANT`. However, this is only a convention and not enforced by the interpreter.

Classes are written in CamelCase in Python. This is just a general agreement, but it is highly recommended to stick to this convention. If a class name consists of several words, they are written together without an underscore. The first letters of each word are always capitalized.

---
[1] https://peps.python.org/pep-0008/

In Python, it is a convention that methods starting with a single underscore are considered private. This means that they are not intended to be used outside of the class. This is just a convention and not enforced by the interpreter. If you want to make a method private, you can start its name with a single underscore, like `_my_private_method`. However, this is only a convention and not enforced by the interpreter.

Here are a few examples how to apply the naming conventions:

```python
# Functions and variables
def add_two_numbers(a, b):
    pass


my_useful_variable = 3.14

# Classes
class MyCar:
    pass
```

> **Comments**
>
> In Python, code after a `#` is ignored by the interpreter. Text after a `#` character is called a comment. Comments are explanations for the reader of the code.
>
> I added some comments to the code here, but I'm not proud of it. I did so only so that you can better understand what the code does. However, this generally is bad practice and should be avoided. You should learn to read code without comments. Good code is self-explanatory and doesn't need comments. Variable and function names should explain the code instead.
>
> Only comment on what the code cannot explain. Only comment on *why* the code does something, not *what* it does.

Now you may work on a project where a different naming convention is used than the one explained here. Don't try to persuade your coworkers to use the naming convention you prefer. It is way too much effort to change all the code, and the benefits of one naming convention compared to another are minor. So just stick to whatever naming convention is used in the project you are working on.

> **Docstrings**
>
> Docstrings are a special kind of comment. They are used to document functions, classes, and modules. Docstrings are written in triple quotes and can be accessed using the `__doc__` attribute. Docstrings are not ignored by the interpreter, but they are not executed either. They are just there for documentation purposes.
>
> One should write docstrings mainly as external documentation. For internal purposes, one should read the code instead.
>
> Docstrings are contrary to comments in some respects, as they are designed to be read by different people. Normal comments are read by the developers who have access to the code. Normal comments should explain *why* the code does something, while docstrings should explain *what* the code does.

Writing Readable Names

Finding good names is one of the hardest tasks in software development. There is no algorithm that tells you how to name things. You have to rely on your intuition and experience. However, there are some general rules that can help you find good names.

The first rule is very simple: if something exists in reality, it should have the same name in your code.

Another important rule is the rule of the least astonishment. This applies not only to naming, but is generally applicable in software development. It would be very surprising if a `car` had a method `fly`. And surprises are never good in software development. Surprises only lead to bugs.

A very difficult question is how long a name should be. This question has no precise answer. Instead, you have to develop a feeling for it. As a rule of thumb, the name of a variable should be long enough that any reader understands what the object is. If you feel the urge to write a whole line for the name of your variable or function, you should probably rethink your code structure. This is a sign that the function contains way too much functionality and should be split into smaller functions. The same applies to classes (p. 67). If a class has too many methods, it should be split into smaller classes. If a function has only one task, it is much easier to find a good name for it.

As we have discussed several times, arguably the most important aspect of code is that every reader can understand it. This means that you have to write code with the reader in mind. Do not use any abbreviations that the reader does not understand. Do not even use abbreviations that the reader might not understand. Code should be as easily readable as possible. This is the most important rule in software development. The few characters you save by using abbreviations are not worth the confusion they cause. Only use abbreviations if they are widely known and used in the industry.

Components of Code

3

In this chapter, we will look at the basic components of code. We will start with variables, which are the most basic building blocks of code. We will then move on to strings, lists, dicts, and tuples. These are the most important data structures in Python and also in any other programming language. We will also look at the basic operations that can be performed on these data structures.

Mutable and Immutable Objects

Mutable objects can be changed after they have been created. You can create a list (p. 20) and change a single value of it. Thus, a list is a mutable object.

```
>>> my_lits = [1,2,3]
>>> my_list[1] = 5
```

Immutable objects, on the other hand, cannot be changed after they have been created. If you try to change the value of an immutable object, you will get an error. You can only reassign the entire object to a new variable. An example of an immutable object is a tuple (p. 32). There is no possibility of changing a single value of a tuple.

Examples of mutable objects in Python are lists and dictionaries. Immutable objects are strings, integers, floats, and tuples.

Mutability might not seem that important to you, but it is of high relevance when dealing with functions (p. 57). Functions can change the value of mutable function arguments, while this is not possible with immutable arguments.

Not being able to change the value of an object is generally a good thing because the caller of the function knows for sure that the argument still has the same value, for example:

```
>>> def add_one(x):
>>>     # do something with x
>>>     pass
>>> my_value = 5
>>> add_one(my_value)
```

© The Author(s), under exclusive license to APress Media, LLC, part of Springer Nature 2026
M. Gähler, *Python Made Easy*,
https://doi.org/10.1007/979-8-8688-2133-2_3

If you call this function `add_one`, do you know what `my_value` is after the function call without knowing the implementation of the function? Yes, you do. It is still 5 because integers are immutable. The value of `my_value` can never be changed when it is used as a function argument.

The whole story changes for immutable objects.

```
>>> def add_one(x):
>>>     # do something with x
>>>     pass
>>> my_list = [5]
>>> add_one(my_value)
```

A list is a mutable object, and therefore, the value of `my_list` can be changed in the function `add_one`. If you want to know what the value of `my_list` is after the function call, you have to look at the implementation of the function. This requires a lot of effort!

On the other hand, it may be that you want to change the value of an object. For immutable objects, you'll have to reassign the entire object to a new variable.

```
>>> def add_one(x):
>>>     return x + 1
>>>
>>> my_value = 5
>>> my_value = add_one(my_value)
```

Now `my_value` is 6, as one would expect.

While in C++, one can choose whether an argument should be mutable or not by using the `const` keyword; in Python, this is not possible. In Python, there are mutable types (lists, dicts, etc.) and immutable types (strings, integers, tuples, etc.), and you'll have to learn how to deal with them.

Assignments

Assignments are very simple, you might think.

```
>>> x = 5
>>> y = x
>>> y
5
```

Now where's the point?

Well, there's more to it. There are cases where you can shoot in your foot with assignments if you don't know what you are doing.

```
>>> x = [1, 2, 3]
>>> y = x
>>> y.append(4)
```

Now, what does this code do? Is `x` now `[1, 2, 3]` or `[1, 2, 3, 4]`? If you run this code, you will immediately see that `x` is now `[1, 2, 3, 4]`. This is because lists are mutable objects (p. 20). The line `y = x` does not create a new list, but rather creates a new reference to the same list. For this reason, any changes that you apply to `y` will also affect `x`.

This is a common source of errors in Python. If you want to create a new list, you have to use the `copy` method.

```
>>> x = [1, 2, 3]
>>> y = x.copy()
```

```
>>> y.append(4)
>>> x
[1, 2, 3]
>>> y
[1, 2, 3, 4]
```

Types

It's a common misconception that Python doesn't have types. This is not true. Python has types, but they are dynamic. This means that you don't have to declare the type of a variable when you create it. Python will automatically assign the type of the variable based on the value that you assign to it. This is different from static typed languages like Java or C++, where you have to declare the type of a variable when you create it. Many programmers regard this as an advantage, as the code becomes much shorter. But at the same time, it also makes it much harder to understand.

Let's assume we have a variable named `my_savings`. We have no idea what this object is. Is it a number? Or a custom class instance? Fortunately, modern IDEs can help us with this. Still, the code would be much simpler to understand, if there was a type declaration.

The behavior of Python is so-called duck typing: if it walks like a duck and it quacks like a duck, then it must be a duck. You don't care what type it is exactly, as long as it supports some specific interfaces. However, this is a very double-edged sword. If you don't know what type an object is, you can't be sure that it supports the interfaces that you expect it to support, especially if you don't have a consistent naming convention.

In Python, you can do pretty much anything you want. One example is to change the type of a variable.

```
>>> x = 5
>>> x = "Hello"
```

And, once again, only because you can do this doesn't mean you should. Assigning a variable to a different value is already bad enough because you'll confuse the reader of your code. If your variable all of a sudden has a different value, it becomes confusing.

Now if your variable all of a sudden has a different type, it gets even worse. You should never reuse variables. If you have to store a new value, you should create a new variable with an appropriate name. And if you think that the other variable already has the perfect name, you should maybe rename that one. There can never be two objects with the same name.

Variables

Variables are a cornerstone in all programming languages. Variables allow us to save values under a specific name and call them up again later. Variables have two properties:

- Variables have a name.
- Variables have a value.

The name of a variable might seem to novices like a detail and is frequently treated as one. This is detrimental. The name of a variable is of utmost importance. You can only deal with objects if they have good names! If you give your variables cryptic names, you won't be able to comprehend your code, as explained in the chapter on names on p. 7.

```
>>> name = "Marco Gähler"
>>> name
'Marco Gähler'
```

Variables can store values. These values can also be overwritten.

```
>>> name = "Marco Gähler"
>>> name
'Marco Gähler'
>>> name = "Donald Duck"
>>> name
'Donald Duck'
```

However, you should always be careful when overriding or changing variables, as this can lead to confusion. In general, it is better to define a new variable for each new purpose and give it an appropriate name. A long time ago, it may have been necessary to save memory by reusing variables, but this is no longer the case. If memory is really an issue, you should be using a more performant programming language than Python.

Variables can not only store text, as can be seen in the previous code examples, but also numbers, entire lists (p. 20), dictionaries (p. 31), or function objects (p. 98).

```
>>> price = 3.50
>>> shopping_list = ["Apples", "Milk", "Eggs"]
```

Global Variables

Let's have a brief look at the following code:

```
>>> name = "Donald Duck"
>>> def print_name():
>>>     print(name)
>>> print_name()
Donald Duck
```

It works as expected. "And what's the point?" you might ask.

To be honest, this code is dreadful. The `name` is a global variable that is used everywhere throughout our short code. And global variables are a bad idea. We have no idea what variables the function `print_name()` depends on, unless we meticulously read the code. Instead, you should write the code as follows:

```
>>> def print_name(name):
>>>     print(name)
>>> print_name("Donald Duck")
Donald Duck
```

It doesn't cost you much to pass the variable as a function argument, but it makes your code much more maintainable and easier to understand. Because the code is much more explicit. It is immediately clear what the function does and what parameters it needs.

The problem with global variables is that they can be changed from anywhere in the code. This is the opposite of encapsulation. It's spaghetti code. I know, at times, it might feel very convenient to use global variables, but it's a very bad idea. Global variables will turn your code into a mess. Trust me, programmers have tried to using global variables since the advent of programming, and it became apparent that it's a very bad idea.

None

None is a special value in Python that represents the absence of a value. It is often used to initialize variables or to indicate that a value has not been set yet.

```
>>> x = None
>>> x
None
```

None is often used if something might have a value, but you don't know it yet. For example, a person might have a death date, but it is not known yet. In the following code example we define a person with a name, age, and a death date, but the death date is not known yet.

```
>>> person = {"name": "John",
    "birth_date": "1990-01-01",
    "death_date": None
}
```

Note that you should avoid using strings as a date format (p. 89). Use the datetime library instead. This code is just for illustration purposes.

Numbers

Numbers are one of the most basic data types in any programming language. Numbers are usually divided into integers and floating point numbers. Integers are whole numbers, while floating point numbers can have a decimal point. When defining a number, Python automatically assigns the correct data type. You can also explicitly define the data type of a number by using the `int()` or `float()` functions.

Floating Point Numbers

Floating point numbers are numbers with a decimal point. However, as for all other programming languages, floating point numbers have a finite precision. It is not possible to represent all real numbers with a finite number of digits. This is a fundamental limitation of floating point numbers in all programming languages, including Python. In order to save memory, Python has a precision of about 15 digits. This is sufficient for most applications, but it can lead to unexpected results in some cases. For example, the following code does not return the expected result:

```
>>> 1 - 2/3
0.33333333333333337
```

Here we have a rounding error because the number 2/3 cannot be represented exactly as a floating point number. This is a fundamental limitation of floating point numbers in all programming languages, including Python. In most cases, you don't have to worry about this, but there are cases where it can lead to very confusing results. There is exactly one thing you have to know about floating point numbers:

> **Never compare floating point numbers for equality!**

Here is an example why:

```
>>> 1 - 2/3 == 1/3
False
```

In fact, it is good that this check fails because we know right away that we shouldn't compare these numbers for equality. Unfortunately, most cases are much harder to spot as they are hidden in the code and they lead to all kind of unexpected results. By far, the worst cases are floating point comparisons that fail sporadically. Let me explain.

In maths, the following equation is true:

$$(a + b) + c = a + (b + c) \tag{3.1}$$

However, this is not true for floating point numbers as rounding errors occur. The following code shows that the order of the operations matters:

```
>>> (1 + 10**-16) + 10**-16 == 1 + (10**-16 + 10**-16)
False
```

Here is the catch: Without the brackets, there is no guarantee in which order these additions are performed. The Python interpreter is free to choose the order of the operations. This means that the result of this code can change depending on the version of Python you are using or even the platform you are running it on. This is a very dangerous situation, as it can lead to bugs that are extremely hard to find.

If you ever have to make a comparison with floating point numbers, you should always use a tolerance value. This means that you check if the difference between the two numbers is smaller than a certain value, for example:

```
>>> abs((1 - 2/3) - 1/3) < 10**-10
True
```

Whenever possible, you should use integers instead of floating point numbers. This is because integers can be represented exactly in Python, while floating point numbers cannot. If you need to work with decimal numbers, you should use the `decimal` module, which provides a way to work with decimal numbers with arbitrary precision. However, I never had to use decimal myself. The correct usage of floating point numbers is sufficient for most applications.

Integers

Example values are 1, 2, and 3, but 0 is also a possible value. Furthermore, negative integers are also possible, such as $-1, -2, -3$, and so on.

While in most other programming languages, integers are limited to a certain range (usually 32 or 64 bit) and nasty bugs occur when they exceed their maximal value. In Python on the other hand, integers can be arbitrarily large. This is because Python uses a special data type for integers that can grow as needed. This is very convenient, but it also means that you have to be careful with performance when working with large integers.

Integers are great, because with integers, you can perform any action with the `+`, `-`, `*`, and `**` operators. That you want and you will always get the expected result. For example, you can add two integers together:

```
>>> 1 + 2
3
```

This also means that you can check them for equality in a fail-safe way:

```
>>> 1 + 2 == 3
True
```

You might wonder what the division operator / does to integers. Apparently, the result of a division is not a whole number, but a fraction, which cannot be represented as an integer. Most other programming languages just round the result to the nearest integer, but Python does it differently. In Python, the / operator always returns a floating point number, even if the result is a whole number. This means that you can use the / operator to divide two integers and get a floating point number as a result. After a division, you are no longer dealing with integers and you are no longer protected against rounding errors. For this reason, it makes sense to adjust your calculations in such a way that you don't use divisions. For example, it makes sense to multiply both sides of the following equation by 3 in order to avoid the division and fix the result.

```
>>> 1/3 + 1/3 == 1 - 1/3
False
>>> 1 + 1 == 3 - 1
True
```

Strings and Numbers

There are many cases where you want to convert a string into a number or vice versa. The most prominent case is input and output, for example, when you read a text file and you want to perform calculations with the numbers in the file. There are many ways how you can deal with these values. However, there is only one "good" way to do it: convert the string to a number as soon as you read it from the file and convert it back to a string when you write it to the file. This way, you can be sure that you are always dealing with numbers and not strings. Of course, there are many ways in Python to perform operations on strings, but this is black magic and should be avoided. Never deal with strings, unless you absolutely have to. Always use dedicated data structures instead.

Booleans

Booleans are a data type that can only have two values: True or False. They are used to represent truth values and are often used in conditional statements (p. 44) to control the flow of the program.

The most commonly used Boolean operators are not, and, and or. These operators can be used to combine or negate Boolean values. Here is what they do:

- not acts on one Boolean value. not negates it. If the value is True, it becomes False and vice versa.
- and acts on two Boolean values. It returns True if both operands are True. Otherwise, it returns False.
- or also acts on two Boolean values. It returns True if at least one of the operands is True. If both operands are False, it returns False.

Here are the results of the Boolean operators for all possible combinations of `True` and `False`:

```
>>> not True
False
>>> not False
True
>>> True and True
True
>>> True and False
False
>>> False and True
False
>>> False and False
False
>>> True or True
True
>>> True or False
True
>>> False or True
True
>>> False or False
False
```

Note that `and` and `or` are symmetric operators. You can swap the two arguments and the result will be the same. For example, `True and False` is the same as `False and True`.

Booleans are very useful for controlling the flow of a program. They are often used in conditional statements to determine whether a certain block of code should be executed or not. For example, you can use a Boolean value to check if a certain condition is met and then execute a block of code accordingly.

Though you have to be very careful with the control flow as it is very prone to errors. This is because humans struggle to understand complex control flows. It is best to keep it as simple as possible. If your code has too many levels of indentation, you should probably rethink your code structure. Excessive usage of Boolean values is a sign that your code is too complex and should be simplified; see also the box on if statements on p. 45.

Lists

Lists, or whatever they are called in other programming languages, are the workhorses of software development. They allow us to store multiple objects in a single variable. This is very useful and probably the most important data structure of all.

Creating Lists

As we have already seen in some cases, Python can be used to store objects with different data types at the same time using lists. While in most other programming languages, such as C++, only objects of one type can be stored (which makes it very efficient), in Python, it is possible to store different objects in a list.

```
>>> a = ["Apple", 5]
```

However, you should avoid doing this at all costs! If you store objects of different data types in a list, the code becomes very confusing. And if you don't believe me, try finding a name for this object.

Lists

You'll have a hard time—a clear sign that your data structure is flawed. Only store objects in lists that have exactly the same properties. We will see how to store different properties of a single object together in the chapter on classes (p. 67).

The simplest list is the empty one containing nothing:

```
>>> empty_list = []
```

The empty list itself is not of much use to us. However, you can now add elements to this list. The most common way to do this is the append function.

```
>>> empty_list.append("hello")
>>> empty_list
['hello']
```

We can repeat this as often as we like. The only limit to the number of elements in the list is the memory space on your computer.

You can also initialize a list containing some elements. This is done by putting the elements in square brackets and separating them with commas.

```
>>> my_list = ["hello", "world"]
>>> my_list
['hello', 'world']
```

> **Old-School Arrays**
>
> You may have heard of arrays, which are used in languages such as C++. In the past, you had to allocate and delete memory yourself in C++ using new and delete if you wanted to create an object at runtime. This was a very fragile and error-prone process. But those days are over once and for all. Even C++ now supports vectors, which have almost the same functionality as lists in Python.

The reverse function to append is pop. Pop removes the last element of a list and returns it.

```
>>> my_list = ["hello"]
>>> my_list.pop()
'hello'
>>> my_list
[]
```

List Comprehensions

A common way to initialize lists in Python is the so-called "list comprehension," where you use the syntax with square brackets.

```
>>> [i**2 for i in range(5)]
[0, 1, 4, 9, 16]
```

range(5) generates the numbers 0 to 4 one after the other, which are stored in the variable i. Then you use i**2, or whatever operation you want to perform with i, to calculate the square of the respective number and save the whole thing in a list. It's best to play around with it a bit to familiarize yourself with list comprehension.

There are also other options for list comprehensions worth mentioning. For example, you can filter a list with a subsequent if statement inside the []. In the following example, we want all the fruits that we have in the corresponding list, except for the pears.

```
>>> fruits = ['apple', 'pear', 'banana']
>>> no_pear = [fruit for fruit in fruits if fruit != "pear"]
>>> no_pear
['apple', 'banana']
```

You can also use list comprehensions to create a list of all the even numbers from 0 to 9.

```
>>> [i for i in range(10) if i % 2 == 0]
[0, 2, 4, 6, 8]
```

Or you can calculate the squares of all the numbers from 0 to 9.

```
>>> [i**2 for i in range(10)]
[0, 1, 4, 9, 16, 25, 36, 49, 64, 81]
```

List comprehensions are very powerful and can be very compact. However, they can also be very difficult to read. So don't go overboard and write a list comprehension that is as complicated as possible. It is always better if the code is a little longer but readable.

Here is a random example of a list comprehension that is a little too long.

```
>>> files = [file.stem.replace(' ', '\ ').strip() for file in
        p.iterdir() if file.is_file() and file.suffix is '.py']
```

Accessing Lists

Accessing elements is one of the most basic operations of lists. As already mentioned, you should write lists where all elements have the same properties. Consequently, you should always iterate over the entire list and perform the same actions for all elements. The code then looks like this:

```
>>> fruits = ["apple", "pear", "banana"]
>>> for fruit in fruits:
...     print(fruit)
...
appple
pear
banana
```

> **English Grammar in Programming**
> It is a common pattern to write something like `for fruit in fruits` in Python. Note that in programming, we don't care about grammar too much. We use the expression `fruits` for a list of fruit, even if the plural of fruit doesn't exist in the English language. But, as we have learned, the goal of programming is to make code easily understandable. Grammatical correctness has low priority here.

With the line `for fruit in fruits:`, we iterate over all elements of the list `fruits` and receive the next element in the variable `fruit`. We then output this element with the line `print(fruit)`.

Sometimes, it may also be useful to receive not only the name of the fruit but also its index in the list. You can use the `enumerate` function for this.

```
>>> for (i, fruit) in enumerate(fruits):
...     print(i, fruit)
...
0 apple
```

```
1 pear
2 banana
```

I have added a bracket around the variables `i, fruit` in the line beginning with `for` to make the syntax a little clearer. You can also leave this out.

Another option, although not as recommended, is the following code:

```
>>> fruits = ["apples", "pears", "bananas"]
>>> for i in range(len(fruits)):
...     print(i, fruits[i])
...
0 apples
1 pears
2 bananas
```

Here we have used a so-called iterator. It is common to use the variable `i` for this purpose. In Python, an iterator is simply a number that you can use to access an element in a list. In general, however, it is recommended not to use iterators. The code is confusing and error-prone. It is better to use the `for ... in ...` syntax.

> **Old-School Loop Iterations**
>
> In C++ and other old-school programming languages, you had to manually assign an iterator to access the elements of an array.
>
> ```
> std::vector<std::string> fruits =
>     {"apple", "pear", "banana"};
> for (int i = 0; i < fruits.size(); i++) {
>     std::cout << fruits[i] << " " << std::endl;
> }
> ```
>
> Or, even worse, you had to use iterators.
>
> ```
> for (std::vector<std::string>::iterator it =
>     fruits.begin(); it != fruits.end(); ++it) {
>     std::cout << *it << " " << std::endl;
> }
> ```
>
> These were very error-prone and confusing ways to access elements of an array because you could easily mess up the comparison or introduce off-by-one errors. Fortunately, these days are over. C++ vectors now also support the `for ... in ...` syntax.

Another way to access elements in a list is the `[]` operator, which we already saw in the previous code example and some of the C++ code. This operator returns the element at a specific index, and it also allows us to change the value at this index. It should be noted that the index starts at 0. The first element in a list, therefore, has the index 0, the second has the index 1, and so on. This is one of the reasons why you should largely avoid indices. You will always mix them up and create errors. Don't use the `[]` operator. If you ever want to use it, your code is probably flawed, and you should fix it.

```
>>> fruits = ["apple", "pear", "banana"]
>>> fruits[1]
'pear'
>>> fruits[1] = "orange"
>>> fruits
['apple', 'orange', 'banana']
```

This code here contradicts the principle that all elements in a list should be treated equally—you simply pick an element from the list at random. For this reason, you should generally avoid using the [] operator. There are usually better ways available to deal with lists.

Accessing Sublists

You can also read a list of elements from a list, as shown in the following example:

```
>>> list = [1,2,3,4,5]
>>> list[1:3]
[2, 3]
```

This operation, also called slicing, may look cool; however, it should only be used sparingly and is a sign of suboptimal code. As we've learned, you shouldn't access random elements in a list with the [] operator, as it is prone to errors and is a sign that not all elements in the list are equal. It is better to write the list in such a way that you can treat all elements equally. If you use slicing, make sure you have plenty of unit tests in place to prevent any off-by-one errors.

As I wrote, I don't like slicing too much. But I have to admit that there are a few useful tricks available for slicing. For example, you can start counting from the back with a negative index. So -1 corresponds to the last element, -2 to the second to last, etc. If you do not specify the start or end of the list, the start or end of the list is automatically used.

```
>>> list = [1,2,3,4,5]
>>> list[-2:]
[4, 5]
>>> list[:-1]
[1, 2, 3, 4]
```

With a third parameter, you can also specify how many elements you want to skip. In this example, every second element in the list is skipped.

```
>>> list = [1,2,3,4,5]
>>> list[::2]
[1, 3, 5]
```

Another useful trick is that you can go through the list backwards with a negative third parameter. You can also skip elements here if you want. However, I'm not going into too much detail as it's a bit confusing. I recommend that you play with the code yourself and see what happens.

```
>>> list = [1,2,3,4,5]
>>> list[::-1]
[5, 4, 3, 2, 1]
```

As a small example, we can check whether a word is a palindrome, i.e., whether it is the same when read forwards and backwards. To do this, we can simply turn the string over and check whether it is the same.

```
>>> word = "anna"
>>> word == word[::-1]
True
```

I have to admit that this code looks cool. But honestly, you should avoid slicing as much as possible. It is a sign of bad code. As I have already said before, you should generally avoid using the [] operator. If you have to splice a list, you should seriously reconsider your code.

Strings vs. Lists

Strings are, roughly speaking, a list of characters and therefore have similar properties to lists. One difference is that strings are immutable. This means that while you can access the individual characters of a string with the [] operator, you cannot change them. Assigning a new value to a character in a string will result in an error.

```
>>> word = "hello"
>>> word[1]
'e'
>>> word[1] = "a"
TypeError: 'str' object does not support item assignment
```

Multidimensional Lists

Lists can also be nested within each other. This is often done to create multidimensional lists, such as matrices. To create a multidimensional list, you have to create a list of lists.

```
>>> matrix = [[1,2,3],[4,5,6],[7,8,9]]
>>> matrix[0]
[1, 2, 3]
>>> matrix[0][1]
2
```

NumPy

Note that for nested lists (Matrices), it is highly advisable to use NumPy (p. 51) due to performance reasons. The only drawback that I'm aware of is that NumPy uses finite precision integers, which can lead to unexpected results if you try to store very large numbers. But for most use cases, this is not a problem.

The first element of the `matrix` (the one with index 0) is a list with elements 1, 2, and 3. The second element of the first element of the `matrix` is 2, etc. It is best to take a look at the following code example and play around with it a bit yourself.

You can also define matrices of higher dimensionality. However, with multiple dimensions, things quickly become confusing.

If you want to make the code more readable, you can also format the input of the `matrix` in the same way as you would with a matrix. Python doesn't care about this, but it is easier to read and should, therefore, be used.

```
>>> matrix = [[1, 2, 3],
...           [4, 5, 6],
...           [7, 8, 9]]
>>> matrix
[[1, 2, 3], [4, 5, 6], [7, 8, 9]]
```

You can also combine the list comprehension with iterating over a list. In the following example, we access the first element of each sublist.

```
>>> matrix = [[1,2,3],[4,5,6],[7,8,9]]
>>> [row[0] for row in matrix]
[1, 4, 7]
```

As already mentioned several times, all elements in a list should have the same properties. It is possible that these lists have different numbers of elements in each row. If this is the case, there is a high probability that you have done something strange, and you should rethink your code.

Lists of lists can also be created in a single line using list comprehension, but this quickly becomes confusing and should, therefore, be avoided.

```
>>> [[[0] * (i + j) for i in range(2)] for j in range(3)]
[[[], [0]], [[0], [0, 0]], [[0, 0], [0, 0, 0]]]
```

The alternative to this is the following code:

```
matrix = []
for j in range(3):
    sub_list = [[0] * (i+j) for i in range(2)]
    matrix.append(sub_list)
print(matrix)
# [[[], [0]], [[0], [0, 0]], [[0, 0], [0, 0, 0]]]
```

You can also create this list without list comprehensions altogether. I think the simple list comprehension is the best solution in this case.

```
matrix = []
for j in range(3):
    sub_list = []
    for i in range(2):
        sub_list.append([0] * (i+j))
    matrix.append(sub_list)
print(matrix)
# [[[], [0]], [[0], [0, 0]], [[0, 0], [0, 0, 0]]]
```

Sorting lists

There are several ways to sort a list. The simplest way is the sort function. This sorts the list in ascending order. If you want to sort the list in descending order, you can set the reverse parameter to True.

```
>>> a = [3,1,2]
>>> a.sort()
>>> a
[1, 2, 3]
>>> a.sort(reverse=True)
>>> a
[3, 2, 1]
```

A slightly modified version of the sort function is the sorted function. This function returns a sorted list without changing the original list.

```
>>> a = [3,1,2]
>>> a_sorted = sorted(a)
>>> a
[3, 1, 2]
>>> a_sorted
[1, 2, 3]
```

Lists

The big question now is whether to use `sort` or `sorted`. The difference between the two functions is apparently rather small. Personally, I prefer `sorted` because it gives me a new list with a new name. As we have already learned, you shouldn't reuse variables. This can lead to confusion if a variable suddenly has different properties. Only use `sort` if you deliberately want to change the original list.

As a side remark, `sorted` can also be used on many other objects, such as strings or dicts, and it always returns a list, for example, a list of sorted keys in the case of the dict.

```
>>> sorted("hello")
['e', 'h', 'l', 'l', 'o']
>>> sorted({1:"2", 4:"5", 3:"11"})
[1, 3, 4]
```

Though this is just some gimmick, you can also use `sorted(list("hello"))` to achieve the same result.

Merging Lists

As you can probably guess, there are different ways to merge lists. The simplest way is the + operator. This joins two lists together.

```
>>> a = [1,2,3]
>>> b = [4,5,6]
>>> a + b
[1, 2, 3, 4, 5, 6]
```

As we have already seen, you can also use the `append` function to add an element to the end of a list. Since we probably don't want to add the whole list, but only the elements of the list, you have to add all the elements of the list one by one.

```
>>> a = [1,2,3]
>>> b = [4,5,6]
>>> for element in b:
...     a.append(element)
...
>>> a
[1, 2, 3, 4, 5, 6]
```

Sometimes, you want to put the first, second, etc., elements of two lists together. For this, Python has the `zip` function. This returns a list of tuples.

```
>>> a = [1,2,3]
>>> b = [4,5,6]
>>> list(zip(a,b))
[(1, 4), (2, 5), (3, 6)]
```

However, you should probably rethink your code if you merge lists. The danger is that you create a list where not all elements are of the same type. Keep different things separate.

How to Continue

> If you don't know it, it's no problem. But if you can't Google it, it is.
> —Wisdom of the internet

We only covered the basics of lists here. There are hundreds of functions that you can use for any possible purpose. There are several different ways to find them. The classical one is reading the documentation, though I wouldn't recommend it. Generally, it's easier to Google what you want to do with lists. This takes some practice to learn the vocabulary of Python, but it's worth it. And then there is the more modern option of using one of the many AI tools. They can help you with your code, but be careful; they can also lead you astray.

The most important conclusion here is that you'll have to practice by yourself. I cannot give you explanations on how to Google or how to use the AI tools. You have to know the names that we learn in this book, and then you can use them to find the functions you need. The most important thing is to practice. You can only learn programming by doing it.

Strings

Strings are text modules used in code. Strings have the property that they always begin and end with quotation marks. Python doesn't care if you use single or double quotes. If you enter a string into the REPL, it will return the string with single quotes. I generally use double quotes as I'm used to them. But it doesn't matter which one you use.

```
>>> "House"
'House'
```

A very important property of strings is the ability to combine text with the contents of other variables. This allows us to generate complex text automatically. There are several syntactical ways to achieve this. The best way is the f-strings introduced with Python 3.8. The syntax of these looks like this:

```
>>> name = "Donald Duck"
>>> f"My name is {name}"
'My name is Donald Duck'
```

So we still have the quotes and closing quotes of the string, but also an `f` at the beginning. Since we want to insert the current value of the variable `name` into the string, we have written `name` within curly brackets. This way, Python knows that `name` is the name of a variable and that it must insert its content into the string.

> **Using of Strings**
>
> Strings should only be used to store text and nothing else. A common antipattern is using strings to store some kind of information akin to a structured object. This is a really bad idea, as it's very prone to errors. If you want to store structured information, you should use a class (p. 67). If strings store simple information, use enums (p. 34) instead. And for saving data, you should use XML, JSON, or a similar file format that is designed to store structured data.

f-strings also work with numbers and even lists. In Python, any object can be converted into a string and thus used in an f-string.

```
>>> shopping_list = ["Apples", "Milk", "Eggs"]
>>> f"Shopping: {shopping_list}"
"Shopping: ['Apples', 'Milk', 'Eggs']"
```

> **Special Characters**
>
> Something you have to be careful with in all programming languages is special characters, such as a line break, \n, a backslash \, or quotation marks. The problem is that these characters are interpreted by the Python interpreter as code and not as part of a string. This is similar to how SQL injection works. There, special characters are also built into a string to inject code into the database. If you ever have to read in text from a user, you should always make sure that all characters are interpreted as a string and never as code. We will not go into this topic any further here. Interested readers will find plenty of literature on the subject on the internet.

There is a simple way to use quotation marks or closing marks in a string: In Python, you can use both single and double quotation marks. If you want to use a single quotation mark in a string, you can use double quotation marks to delimit the string, and vice versa.

```
>>> "He said 'what?'"
"He said 'what?'"
```

Various Types of Strings

The standard strings we just got to know are sometimes not appropriate for several reasons. The most common issues are that you want to define a string that spans multiple lines or you have to use many special characters. For this, Python has different types of strings, of which I will explain only the most common ones.

The first type is, as we have already seen, the f-string. f-strings are used to insert the current value of a variable into a string. This is done by putting the variable name in curly brackets. The f-string is defined by an f in front of the string.

```
>>> fruit_name = "Apple"
>>> quantity = 10
>>> f"I have {quantity} {fruit_name} in stock."
'I have 10 Apple in stock.'
```

The second type is the multiline string. This is defined by three quotation marks at the beginning and end of the string. This way, you can write a string that spans over many lines.

```
>>> multiline_string = """This is a multiline string.
... It spans over many lines."""
>>> print(multiline_string)
This is a multiline string.
It spans over many lines.
```

The third type of string that we have a look at is the raw string. This is defined by an r in front of the string. This way, you can write a string without having to escape special characters.

```
>>> raw_string = r"Here is a \n"
>>> print(raw_string)
Here is a \n
```

String Operations

There are many helpful operations that can be performed on strings. As a rule of thumb, a string is a list of single characters, and you can do almost anything with a string that you can do with a list. As with lists, you should always reconsider if you have to use these operations.

First of all, you can concatenate strings using the + operator.

```
>>> "Hello " + "World"
'Hello World'
```

You can also multiply strings with the * operator. While it is funny, it is not particularly useful.

```
>>> "Hello " * 3
'Hello Hello Hello '
```

You can also access individual characters in a string using the [] operator. The index starts at 0. The first character in a string has the index 0, the second has the index 1, etc.

```
>>> "Hello"[1:3]
'el'
```

Another operation we know from lists is iterating over all elements with the for ... in syntax.

```
>>> for letter in "Hello":
...     print(letter)
...
H
e
l
l
o
```

An operation that is really useful is the split function. It breaks up a string at a certain character and returns a list of the individual parts. This is used if you want to read a CSV file, for example.

```
>>> "1,2,3,4".split(",")
['1', '2', '3', '4']
>>> "Hello World".split(" ")
['Hello', 'World']
```

Another useful method is the contains function. It checks if a string contains a certain character and returns a Boolean value.

```
>>> "Hello".contains("l")
True
>>> "Hello".contains("x")
False
```

There are dozens of other operations that can be performed on strings. You can find them in the documentation.

Meanwhile, some of these operations can be very useful; you also have to be careful not to overdo it. Strings should be processed right away when you read them. The rest of the code shouldn't contain any string logic. Never.

Dicts

Dictionaries (dicts for short; in other languages also called hashmaps or maps) are another very useful data structure. Dicts allow us to save values under a specific name. This can be done dynamically, i.e., at runtime, in contrast to the definition of normal variables, which have to be defined when you write the code. Dicts are therefore very useful if you want to read in a file with a lot of information at runtime and save it in a sorted manner. An example of this is the following code:

```
>>> recipes = {}
>>> recipes["Pizza"] = ["Dough", "tomatoes", "cheese"]
>>> recipes
{'Pizza': ['Dough', 'tomatoes', 'cheese']}
```

Note that the key can be pretty much anything; it doesn't have to be a string.

```
>>> numbers = {1: "one", 2: "two"}
>>> numbers[1]
'one'
```

We can iterate over all elements in a dict. This can be done using both the keys (key) and the values (value).

```
>>> recipes["Pasta"] = ["Penne", "tomatoes"]
>>> recipes
{'Pizza': ['Dough', 'tomatoes', 'cheese'],
'Pasta': ['Penne', 'tomatoes']}
>>> for recipename in recipes:
...     print(recipename)
...
Pizza
Pasta
>>> for recipename in recipes:
...     print(recipe[recipename])
...
['Dough', 'tomatoes', 'cheese']
['Penne', 'tomatoes']
```

We can also iterate over the values of a dict directly by using the `values()` function.

```
>>> for recipe_ingredients in recipes.values():
...     print(recipe_ingredients)
...
['Dough', 'tomatoes', 'cheese']
['Penne', 'tomatoes']
```

What you ultimately need, be it the values or the keys, must be determined individually in each case. All I can tell you is that dicts are very powerful and an enormously useful tool. How and for what else you can use them would go beyond the scope of this book.

There is a joke saying that dicts are the solution to all LeetCode problems. This is not entirely true, but it is a good indication of how important dicts are.

A common example is the use of dictionaries to count the frequency of words in a text, as shown in the following code.

```
text = "This is a test. This is only a test."

word_counts = {}
for word in text.split():
```

```
    if word in word_counts:
        word_counts[word] += 1
    else:
        word_counts[word] = 1
print(word_counts)
# {'This': 2, 'is': 2, 'a': 2, 'test.': 2, 'only': 1}
```

The code snippet

```
if word in word_counts:
    word_counts[word] += 1
else:
    word_counts[word] = 1
```

is worth remembering. It is a common pattern to count things that you don't know in advance.

It is also worth mentioning that dicts offer great performance, and the lookup time is, on average, constant with regard to the dict size. This is very important and generally allows you to use dicts in performance-critical tasks!

On the other hand, I have never encountered a case where a dictionary was so huge that it could become the bottleneck of some algorithm.

Tuples

Tuples are another data structure that is used very frequently in Python, though they are very inconspicuous. Tuples are very similar to lists, with the difference that they are immutable; they cannot change their value. A tuple is, simply put, a combination of several values. Tuples are often used as function arguments or return values.

The basic syntax of using a tuple looks like this:

```
>>> a = (2,1)
>>> a
(2, 1)
```

You can reassign a to a new value, but you cannot change the value of the tuple itself. With the [] operator, you can access elements of a tuple, but not change them as tuples are immutable.

```
>>> a = (1,2)
>>> a[0]
1
>>> a[0] = 4
Traceback (most recent call last):
  File "<stdin>", line 1, in <module>
TypeError: 'tuple' object does not support item assignment
```

A function that returns a tuple is the divmod function, which returns the integer quotient and the remainder of a division.

```
>>> divmod(10, 3)
(3, 1)
```

Here both (10,3) and (3,1) form a tuple. Tuples themselves are like a container that contains several objects. However, tuples are only really useful when you can read these values again. To do this, you simply "unpack" tuples into variables.

Tuples

```
>>> a = divmod(10, 3)
>>> quotient, rest = a # Unpacking the tuple
>>> quotient
3
```

You can also save yourself the intermediate step with the variable a and unpack the tuple directly.

```
>>> quotient, rest = divmod(10, 3)
>>> quotient
3
```

You can, of course, also write your own functions that return tuples. Here is an example of a function that takes the length and width of a rectangle and returns the area and perimeter. Note that it's optional to add brackets around the return values area, perimeter.

```
def rectangle(length, width):
    area = length * width
    perimeter = 2 * (length + width)
    return area, perimeter
area, perimeter = rectangle(3, 4)
print(area) # 12
```

In the line that calls the rectangle function, the tuple is unpacked directly into the variables area and perimeter. Here you can write area, perimeter with or without brackets. The same applies to the return statement within the function.

If you use tuples, you should be careful that they do not become too large. Otherwise, it is very easy to lose track. Also, returning a tuple may be an indication that your function or method is doing too much. When in doubt, always return one single value.

Tuples vs. Lists

Tuples and lists are very similar. In Python, they can both store different objects.

```
>>> my_list = [1, "hello", [2, 3, 4]]
>>> my_list[1]
'hello'
>>> my_tuple = (1, "hello", [2, 3, 4])
>>> my_tuple[1]
'hello'
```

But they also have differences. Most notably, tuples are immutable. Trying to change one element results in a TypeError.

```
>>> my_tuple = (1, "hello", [2, 3, 4])
>>> my_tuple[1] = "bla"
Traceback (most recent call last):
  File "<stdin>", line 1, in <module>
TypeError: 'tuple' object does not support item assignment
```

Lists and tuples have very distinct applications. It is recommended to store objects in a list if they all have the same properties in order to iterate over them. Tuples, on the other hand, may contain different objects. Though it also has to be said that I advise against passing around tuples. If you want to store different objects, you should rather create a class. For this reason, I hardly ever use tuples.

Enums

A common problem in software development is that you want to store and use different colors, for example. Let's say we only want to use red, blue, and green. Now we can write the following code:

```
favoritecolor = "blue"
if favoritecolor == "blue":
    # ...
```

This is absolutely correct code. However, it has the problem of being error-prone. You can make a typo and write blu. This will have completely unpredictable consequences, and the result will probably be wrong. The computer cannot warn you because it does not know that blu is the result of a typo. Of course, you can argue that you are working carefully, but this code is and will remain error-prone. Error-prone code should be avoided at all costs.

The best option is to define a so-called enum (the short form for enumeration).

```
from enum import Enum
class Color(Enum):
    RED = 1
    GREEN = 2
    BLUE = 3
```

The corresponding code is

```
favoritecolor = Color.BLUE
```

and if you need the value associated with BLUE, you can access it with the code `favoritecolor.value`.

You might now be wondering what might happen if you make a typo:

```
favoritecolor = color.BLU
```

This returns the following error message:

```
AttributeError: BLU. Did you mean: 'BLUE'?
```

This is infinitely better than the unpredictable behavior if you misspell a string. You even get a very clear error message telling you where the problem lies.

The only "disadvantage" of enums is that you have to know all the possible values in advance. If you don't know all the possible colors at the time of programming, you can't use an enum.

> **About Enums**
> Enums are great, but many programmers don't know about them. Whenever you have a predefined selection of values, you should use an enum. Avoid using strings, as this is error-prone.

Rarely Used Data Structures

There are many more data structures that I would like to introduce for the sake of completeness, though I rarely use them myself.

Sets

A set is similar to a list, but all entries are unique. If you add the same value twice, it will only be stored once. I don't use sets often, but they can be useful. Here are some code examples of how you can use sets. Note that it is not possible to access elements in a set by index.

```
>>> a = {1,2,3}
>>> a
{1, 2, 3}
>>> a.add(1)
>>> a
{1, 2, 3}
>>> len(a)
3
>>> for element in a:
...     print(element)
...
1
2
3
>>> 1 in a
True
```

The following is a neat piece of code to check if all elements in a list are unique:

```
>>> def has_all_unique_elements(mylist):
>>>     return len(set(mylist)) == len(mylist)
>>>
>>> has_all_unique_elements([1, 2, 3])
True
>>> has_all_unique_elements([1, 2, 3, 1])
False
```

Exceptions

To throw (in python also called to raise) an exception is a common thing to do when something goes wrong in the code. A simple example is the code `1./0.`. The result of this calculation is not defined from a purely mathematical point of view. Some programming languages return `inf` (infinite) or `NaN` (Not a Number) as the result. Python, on the other hand, throws an exception.

```
>>> 1./0.
Traceback (most recent call last):
File "<stdin>", line 1, in <module>
ZeroDivisionError: float division by zero
```

In this case, it is a `ZeroDivisionError`, and the associated message is "float division by zero". Exceptions are usually thrown when the code is in an invalid state, and Python itself does not know how to deal with it, for example, when it cannot open a file because it does not exist, when it should call a function that is not defined, or when there are syntax errors. Python tries to tell you as precisely as possible what is going wrong and where exactly so that you can fix the error.

It is also very helpful if you define your own exceptions. Let's assume you are writing software where the user has to enter his salary. Since you work diligently and you're a smart programmer, you know that the user could come up with the idea of entering a negative salary. Depending on what your code does exactly, this could have unforeseeable consequences. It makes no sense to have a negative salary. To prevent this, it is best to raise an exception if the salary is negative.

```
>>> def form(salary):
...     if salary < 0:
...         raise Exception("Salary must not be negative")
...
>>> form(-1)
Traceback (most recent call last):
File "<stdin>", line 1, in <module>
File "<stdin>", line 3, in form
Exception: Salary must not be negative
```

Try, Catch, Else, Finally

If you know that a certain piece of code might throw an exception, you can use the `try-except` block to catch the exception and handle it gracefully. This way, your program does not crash, and you can inform the user about the problem. The code of a try-catch block looks roughly like this:

```
try:
    # Code that might throw an exception
    risky_function()
except Exception as e:
    # Code to handle the exception
    print(f"An error occurred: {e}")
```

You put a function that could raise an exception into a try block and then catch the exception in the except block. The variable `e` contains the exception that was thrown, and you can use it to print a message or log the error.

In Python, there is the additional possibility to execute code if no exception was thrown using the `else` block. The `else` block is executed only if the code in the `try` block did not throw an exception. This is useful if you want to execute some code that should only run if everything went fine.

```
try:
    # Code that might throw an exception
    risky_function()
except Exception as e:
    # Code to handle the exception
    print(f"An error occurred: {e}")
else:
    # Code that runs if no exception was thrown
    print("Everything went fine!")
```

Furthermore, there is the `finally` block, which is executed regardless of whether an exception was thrown or not. This is useful for cleanup tasks, such as closing files or releasing resources.

```
try:
    file = open('file.txt', 'r')
    data = file.read()
except IOError:
```

```
        print("Error reading file")
finally:
    file.close()
```

When to Use Exceptions

Exceptions should be used to handle errors that are not expected during normal operation. They are not meant to be used for control flow, i.e., you should not use exceptions to handle cases that you expect to happen regularly. For example, if you want to check if a file exists before opening it, you should not use an exception. Instead, you can use the `os.path.exists` function to check if the file exists. Vice versa, the `open` function raises an exception if the file it's supposed to open does not exist. Of course, one could return a flag that indicates whether the file was opened successfully or not, but this isn't done as the resulting syntax would be too complicated. Raising an exception is much more common.

The harder question is where you should catch the exception. As a rule of thumb, you should catch an exception at the location where you can deal with it.

In the following code, we have a function that divides two numbers. If the divisor is zero, it raises a `ZeroDivisionError`. In the `main` function, we catch this exception and print an error message. This way, we can handle the error gracefully without crashing the program.

```
def div(dividend, divisor):
    return dividend / divisor

def main():
    dividend = int(input("Enter dividend: "))
    divisor = int(input("Enter divisor: "))
    try:
        result = div(dividend, divisor)
        print(f"Result: {result}")
    except ZeroDivisionError as e:
        print("You cannot divide by zero!")
    except ValueError as e:
        print("Invalid input. Please enter a number.")
```

There are also different ways to handle this problem. For example, you could check that the divisor is not zero before calling the `div` function. This would be a way to avoid the exception altogether. However, it is not always possible to get around exceptions. In many cases, it is not so obvious what the potential exceptions depend on and you'll only know during the execution of the program if an exception is thrown or not. In this case, you have to catch the exception at the point where you can handle it.

Pitfalls

Exceptions are a very powerful tool, yet they also have some serious drawbacks. One problem of exceptions is that they are not apparent in the function signature. This is a serious issue. You'll only know if a function throws an exception if you read the documentation (if it exists) or all the code of the function (which can be extremely long).

In Java, there was the attempt to solve this problem by introducing checked exceptions. This means that the compiler checks if you catch all exceptions that a function can throw. This is not the case in Python, and it is also not planned to be introduced. The reason for this is that it would make the code more complicated and less readable. In Python, it is up to the programmer to read the documentation and understand which exceptions can be thrown.

Custom Exceptions

Exceptions describe something like the type of problem that is involved. The text in them is a precise description. To filter the types of problems, you can also define special exceptions. To do this, you must inherit from the class `exception`, as shown in the following code for `MyException`.

```
>>> class MyException(Exception):
...     pass
...
>>> def form(salary):
...     if salary < 0:
...         raise MyException("Salary may not be negative")
...
>>> form(-1)
Traceback (most recent call last):
File "<stdin>", line 1, in <module>
File "<stdin>", line 3, in form
MyException: Salary may not be negative
```

When an exception is thrown, you usually don't want the whole program to crash just to tell you that something didn't go quite as expected. If the operating system can't save a file because your hard drive is full, you'd expect an error message instead of a crash of your computer. To prevent the exception from crashing the whole system, you can implement a so-called `try-catch` block. This block executes code that might throw an exception and catches it. The code for this looks like this:

```
>>> try:
...     1/0
... except:
...     print("Division by 0")
...
Division by 0
```

Here, the code `1/0` in the `try` block raised an exception as expected. This was caught by the `except` block, and as a result, the `print` command was executed.

As I already mentioned, we now want to sort the different exceptions and react differently depending on the type of exception. To do this, we need to define several `except` blocks and catch a specific type of exception in each one.

```
class MyException(Exception):
    pass

try:
    1/0
except MyException as e:
    print('Invalid input')
    print(e)
except Exception as e:
    print('Unknown problem. Please contact the support.')
    print(e)
```

The output of this code is

```
Unknown problem. Please contact the support.
division by zero
```

Here the division `1/0` throws a `ZeroDivisionError`. `MyException` is not of this type, so the corresponding `except` block is ignored. The exception is only caught and processed by the second `except` block, since all exceptions in Python are of type `Exception` by default.

To ensure that your software catches all exceptions and does not suddenly crash because of them, it is worth putting the entire code into a single `try-except` block.

```
try:
    main()
except MyException as e:
    print('Invalid input. Fix your input and try again.')
    print(e)
except Exception as e:
    print('Unknown problem. Please contact the support.')
    print(e)
```

By distinguishing between specific exceptions (`MyException`) and general exceptions (`Exception`), you can also distinguish between exceptions that you have deliberately thrown and those that you did not expect. In the former, the user has done something wrong; in the latter, you have overlooked a possible problem.

Code Structure

Most novices write code without any structure. They are busy trying to get the code to work and don't think about structure. This is a big mistake. If you structure your code well, you will save yourself a lot of time in the long run.

> **Complexity of Code**
> The complexity of your code should only be as high as that of the problem you are trying to solve. If the complexity of your code is much higher, you should rethink the structure of your code.

It is not possible to give you a one-rule-fits-all solution. But there are some general rules that will make your life easier.

Most important of all, your code should represent the problem you are trying to solve, though it shouldn't be a one-to-one representation of real life. Just like a computer game doesn't have to be a one-to-one representation of the real world, having a game with a simplified model of reality is generally better than trying to model the real world. You should implement only the parts of the problem that are necessary to solve it. You have to abstract the problem to the bare minimum.

You should be able to talk about your problems with the people from the marketing team. You should be using exactly the same expressions as they do. And these expressions should have exactly the same properties as in your code. For example, if you're in the car business, you should probably have a `Car` class. If you care about the parts of the car, the `engine`, `tires`, etc., should probably be member variables of the `Car` class, as they are parts of the car.

On the other hand, you could only be interested in selling cars. In this case, you don't need to care about the internals of a car. The `car` object only has a variable `price` and maybe some additional options.

> **Cyclic Dependencies**
> It is important that you never have any cyclic dependencies in your code. Cyclic dependencies are an antipattern and will make your code very hard to understand. For example, your `car` contains an `engine` as a member variable. This also means that the `engine` shouldn't know anything about the surrounding `car`. You can access the engine only through the `car` object, and this is a good thing. In reality, you can access the engine only through the car, so it shouldn't be any different in your code.

> **Formatting**
> Code formatting is another important aspect of software development. Well-formatted code is easier to read and understand. This applies not only to software, of course, but to any text. We can learn something from newspapers and books here.
>
> Text is easier to read when the lines are not too long. If lines are too long, this is also a sign that there is too much complexity in a single line. PEP 8, therefore, recommends a maximum line length of "only" 79 characters. This was also the case with the Linux kernel, which is written in C, and the length of the tabs is 8 spaces. This *forces* you to structure and simplify the code. This is also the thinking of Linus Torvalds, the main developer of Linux: "if you need more than 3 levels of indentation, you're screwed anyway, and should fix your program."
>
> There are also standards that allow slightly longer lines. 100 characters per line is a common standard. But the lines definitely shouldn't be longer than that.

There are different tools, so-called linters, that check your code for formatting errors. The most common one is `pylint`. It checks your code for formatting errors and also for other problems. It is a good idea to use it regularly. You can also integrate it into your IDE, so you don't have to run it manually. A more modern and especially faster alternative at the time of writing this book is `Ruff`.

Coupling and Cohesion

> **Coupling and Cohesion**
> Reduce coupling and increase cohesion.

Coupling is a measure of how much the different parts of your code depend on each other. Coupling is an inevitable evil, as code couldn't exist without it. Coupling is like the glue that holds everything together. But too much glue makes everything sticky, and your code becomes hard to change. So, you should introduce as little coupling as possible.

Code Structure

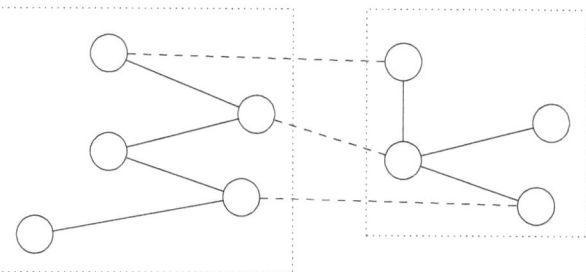

Fig. 3.1 Graphical representation of a system with strong coupling (many dashed lines between objects) and low cohesion (few lines within objects)

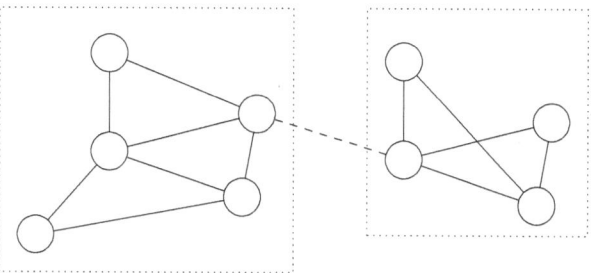

Fig. 3.2 Graphical representation of a system with weak coupling and high cohesion

Cohesion refers to whether different parts of the code belong together. This expression is used mostly for classes and serves as a rule of thumb for how you should structure them. You should increase cohesion by removing everything from a class that doesn't belong there. This is a good way to improve the quality of your code. According to the SRP, classes should do only one thing. If you increase cohesion by removing things from the class, you automatically converge toward the state where a class does only one thing.

An abstract way to think about coupling and cohesion is shown in Figures 3.1 and 3.2. You can think of each dotted box as one object, each circle is one element (e.g. a variable or a function) and the solid and dashed lines are dependencies. The goal is to have many dependencies within each object, while reducing the number of dependencies between different objects, as seen in Figure 3.2.

Loops and If Statements

4

Loops and if statements are two of the most important concepts in software development. They allow the code to not only be executed linearly from top to bottom but also to branch and repeat. For and if statements control the flow of a program.

Loops

The best programmers are lazy. They only do something when it is required. Without a clear goal in mind, they do nothing at all. And if something has to be done multiple times, they don't write the code multiple times (and no, they don't copy it either). They write a function and put it in a for loop. Here is an example:

```
>>> print("hello hello hello ")
hello hello hello
```

So we output the same expression three times in a row. This can be done better. We can simplify this by using a so-called for loop.

```
>>> for _ in range(3):
...     print("hello", end=" ")
...
hello hello hello
```

So we now output "hello" three times in a row. We also had to adjust the end character. Normally, a print call is followed by a line break. But here, we only wanted to have a lesson, so we inserted the code end=" " to suppress this behavior.

Furthermore, we can also use the counter of the for loop and work with it. A simple example is the following:

```
>>> even_numbers = [0, 2, 4, 6, 8]
```

One of the many ways to create this list is to use a for loop.

```
>>> even_numbers = []
>>> for i in range(5):
...     even_numbers.append(2*i)
...
>>> even_numbers
[0, 2, 4, 6, 8]
```

Or, as we have learned in the section on lists, we can also use list comprehension.

```
>>> even_numbers = [2*i for i in range(5)]
>>> even_numbers
[0, 2, 4, 6, 8]
```

With for loops, we can also iterate over lists.

```
>>> for fruit in ["apple", "pear", "banana"]:
...     print(fruit)
...
apple
pear
banana
```

This is an enormously useful way of accessing all elements of a list one after the other and is therefore a very common technique. This way of accessing elements of a list is now established in most other programming languages. In the past, for example, in C++, you always had to deal with the index of the list, which is prone to errors because you can easily make a mistake by one.

For loops are also very closely linked to the range() function. As we have already seen, the following code section is also widely used:

```
>>> for i in range(3):
...     print(i)
...
0
1
2
```

Nested Loops

Loops can also be nested one inside the other. This is a common pattern and is used when you have to iterate over a two-dimensional list.

```
for i in range(3):
    for j in range(3):
        print(i, j)
# prints
# 0 0
# 0 1
# etc.
```

However, you have to be careful with nesting for loops, as it makes the code hard to understand. If you have a three-dimensional object, it may be justified to nest three for loops for the different dimensions. But you shouldn't put any more logic in this loop, as it is already hard to understand.

If Statements

If statements, like classes, are both a blessing and a curse. They are undoubtedly very useful but also very dangerous. But let's start from the beginning.

An if statement is used so that we can distinguish between different cases. For example, we can write a function that takes a speed as an argument and warns us if it is over 60. Instead of the variable name speed, I used the physical formula symbol v.

```
>>> def speed_limit(v):
...     if v > 60:
...         print("You're driving too fast!")
...
>>> speed_limit(61)
You're driving too fast!
```

> **The Danger of If Statements**
>
> If statements are useful but also dangerous. Lines that contain an if statement are much more likely to contain an error than lines without an if statement. This is simply because people have difficulty dealing with such logic. Since software development is mainly about people and not, as you might expect, about computers, we have to write the code so that people make as few errors as possible. In other words, we have to write code that contains as few if statements as possible.

There are various ways to avoid `if` statements. But I can only show you the door; you have to go through it on your own.

The most common way is so-called polymorphism (p. 97). This allows you to create different objects that have different properties, as we'll see in the chapter on classes (p. 67) and the section on dependency injection (p. 97). We can store cars and spaceships in the same list, even though they sometimes have very different properties. But as long as they support the same interface, these objects are interchangeable.

Another way to avoid if statements is with range-based for loops:

```
cars = ["BMW", "Audi", "Mercedes"]
for car in cars:
    print(car)
```

Like this, we avoided all if statements that "classical" for loops would have.

With range-based for loops, you also don't have to worry about empty lists. If you iterate over an empty list, nothing happens. This is most likely the behavior you want. With other for loops, you might first have to check if the list is empty, a common source of bugs.

Nested If Statements

If statements can be nested one inside the other. This is a common pattern and is used when you have to distinguish between different cases. Here is an example:

```
>>> def speed_limit(v, is_drunk):
...     if v > 60:
...         print("You're driving too fast!")
...         if is_drunk:
...             print("And you're also drunk!")
...
>>> speed_limit(61, True)
You're driving too fast!
And you're also drunk!
```

> **Nested If Statements**
> In theory, there is nothing wrong with nested if statements. The computer doesn't struggle to execute them, and it is possible to write nested if statements correctly. But you might already see the issue. We don't write code theoretically. Code is written by and for people, and people make mistakes. People make particularly many mistakes with if statements. For this reason, one should avoid if statements, and one should certainly avoid nested if statements. They are simply too error-prone.

Boolean Logic

Boolean logic deals with the values `True` and `False` and how they can be combined using the logical operators `and`, `or`, and `not`. The combination of these operators and values can be represented in a truth table.

The truth tables can be read as follows: Given a value A (and maybe B), what is the result of the logical operation? For example, if `A=True`, then `not A` is `False`.

In Python, the use of logical operators looks like this:

```
>>> True and False
False
>>> True or False
True
>>> not True
False
```

Variables in Python can also be converted into Boolean values. Elements that are either 0 or empty are converted to `False`. Everything else is converted to `True`.

```
>>> bool(0)
False
>>> bool(1)
True
>>> bool("")
False
>>> bool("a")
True
>>> bool([])
False
>>> bool([0])
True
```

One can also use the implicit conversion of variables to Boolean values in if statements.

```
if x:
    print("x exists")
```

You always have to be extra careful when using logical operators, as they are also quite error-prone. On the other hand, using logical operators is still better than nesting if statements. Make sure that logical operations are written as clearly as possible. If you have to think about what the code does, you should rewrite it. And always consider: the best code has no if statements at all.

Return, Break, and Continue

Return, break, and continue are three important concepts used in loops and if statements. Return is used to exit a function and return a result. Break is used to exit a loop, and continue is used to end the current loop iteration and continue to the next one.

Though early returns, breaks, and continues should be used very sparingly, they are a sign of bad code because not all elements of a list are treated equally and, therefore, a sign that your code is flawed. If you use an early return, break, or continue, you should ask yourself if you can't write the code better. In most cases, you can.

Return

Return is a very simple concept. It is used to exit a function and return a result. Here is a simple example:

```
def search_two():
    for i in range(5):
        if i == 2:
            return i

print(search_two()) # prints 2
```

When the iterator i is 2, the code reaches the return statement and then aborts. The iterations for i = 3 and 4 are not executed.

While early returns in if statements are generally considered useful, you shouldn't use them in for loops because all elements of a list are supposed to be treated equally. If you use an early return, this is apparently not the case.

Break

Break is used to end a loop.

```
for i in range(5):
    print(i)
    if i == 3:
        break
# prints: 0 1 2 3
```

Break has two differences from return. First, it does not end the function (it doesn't even have to be inside one), only the loop. Second, it does not return a value.

Continue

Continue is used to end the current loop iteration and continue with the next one. So in this code, continue is used to skip the number 3.

```
for i in range(5):
    if i == 3:
        continue
    print(i)
# prints: 0 1 2 4
```

Basic Mathematics

Solid knowledge of mathematics and logical thinking is, without a doubt, the foundation of any piece of software. This is why scientists and engineers have the potential to be good software engineers.

The syntax for mathematical operations is different in every programming language. So even if you know, say, C++, you'll still have to learn a few details about Python. There are some details where Python zigs while other programming languages zag.

Basic Mathematics with Python

Arithmetic Operations

Let's start with subtraction and addition. Here, everything is as you would expect.

```
>>> 8 + 3
11
>>> 9 - 5
4
```

Also, the multiplication is as you would expect.

```
>>> 3 * 15
15
```

However, the division returns a somewhat unexpected result.

```
>>> 5/2
2.5
```

In many other programming languages, the result of this line would be 2, since it is an integer division, and the result must therefore be an integer. In Python, however, this is a little different. To calculate integer division, you have to use the // operator in Python:

```
>>> 5//2
2
```

And for the sake of completeness, here is the modulus operator %, which is used to calculate the remainder of a division.

```
>>> 5 % 2
1
```

Integer division and the modulus operator are very important in discrete mathematics. These operations are used in cryptography, among other things.

For the power operator, Python uses the ** sign.

```
>>> 2**3
8
>>> 9**0.5
3.0
```

The Math Module

For more complicated functions, there is the mathematics library. This library defines trigonometric functions such as sine and cosine. To use this library, we must first import it.

```
>>> import math
>>> math.cos(0)
1.0
```

There are several different ways of importing something. With the above syntax of `import math`, you always have to use the prefix `math.` afterwards. This may bother you, but it is quite useful because you always know where a certain function comes from. There are also the following alternatives:

```
>>> from math import *
>>> cos(0)
1.0

>>> from math import cos
>>> cos(0)
1.0
```

Though the first option is generally not recommended because it makes it unclear where the `cos` function was defined. If you look at the corresponding line `cos(0)` in the code, it is likely that the function `cos` was defined by the user. It is often not as clear as in this code that the function originates from the `math` library.

Another possibility is the following:

```
>>> import math as m
>>> m.cos(0)
1.0
```

In general, however, this way of importing libraries is not recommended. Choose names for your libraries that are short enough that you do not need to abbreviate them. Only use abbreviations for libraries where it is a common practice to do so. Two examples are NumPy and matplotlib:

```
>>> import numpy as np
>>> import matplotlib.pyplot as plt
```

We will also often use these two libraries in the following sections to calculate things and display them graphically.

NumPy

NumPy is the most important library for numerical calculations in Python. It is used in most scientific fields and has a lot of functionality implemented. Numpy allows you to write high-performance code, as it is written in C and is therefore much faster than ordinary Python code.

One thing numpy is useful for is generating numbers with equal spacing.

```
>>> np.linspace(1, 3, 5)
array([1. , 1.5, 2. , 2.5, 3. ])
```

A somewhat cumbersome alternative to this would be to create a list "by hand" that has the same values.

```
>>> [i/10 for i in range(10, 35, 5)]
[1.0, 1.5, 2.0, 2.5, 3.0]
```

In my opinion, this is much harder to read.

Matrices

Numpy has pretty much every conceivable function for matrices implemented. Let's first define a matrix.

```
>>> m = np.matrix([[1, 2], [3, 4]])
>>> m
matrix([[1, 2],
        [3, 4]])
```

Now we can calculate the transpose or the inverse of this matrix:

```
>>> m.getT()
matrix([[1, 3],
        [2, 4]])
>>> from numpy.linalg import inv
>>> inv(m)
matrix([[-2. , 1. ],
        [ 1.5, -0.5]])
```

We can also multiply natural numbers with matrices or matrices with each other:

```
>> 3*m
matrix([[ 3, 6],
        [ 9, 12]])
>>> m*inv(m)
matrix([[1.0000000e+00, 0.0000000e+00],
        [8.8817842e-16, 1.0000000e+00]])
```

When multiplying the matrix, it should be noted that Python returns a value that is not exactly 0, as it is limited by the accuracy of the calculation.

We can also calculate the eigenvalues (EW) and eigenvectors (EV) of the matrix.

```
>>> import numpy.linalg as LA
>>> EW, EV = LA.eig(m)
```

Using the eigenvectors, the matrix A can be put into diagonal form.

```
>>> LA.inv(EV)*m*EV
matrix([[-3.72281323e-01,  8.23749941e-16],
[ 3.53579641e-16,  5.37228132e+00]])
```

As expected, the matrix is now in an (almost) diagonal form, and the diagonal entries are the eigenvalues of the matrix. The nondiagonal entries are very close to 0, but not exactly 0. This is due to the limited accuracy of the calculation.

```
>>> EW
array([-0.37228132,  5.37228132])
```

Images

One application of matrices is images. In images, every pixel is a value and the pixels are ordered in a matrix. This sounds like a perfect application for numpy, doesn't it?

Indeed, let's have a look. Let's start with creating a sample image from a numpy array.

```
import imageio.v2 as imageio
import numpy as np

# Create a 200x200 RGB image with a gradient
height, width = 200, 200
image_array = np.zeros((height, width, 3), dtype=np.uint8)

# Create a gradient from blue to red
for i in range(height):
    for j in range(width):
        image_array[i, j] = \
            [i * 255 // height, 0, j * 255 // width]

imageio.imwrite("gradient_image.png", image_array)
```

The output of this code is shown in Figure 5.1.

Fig. 5.1 An image created from a numpy array with a gradient from blue to red

(a) (b)

Fig. 5.2 Some manipulated Apress logos. (**a**) The Apress logo. (**b**) The Apress logo flipped vertically

(a) (b)

Fig. 5.3 Some more manipulated Apress logos. (**a**) The Apress logo flipped horizontally. (**b**) The Apress logo rotated 90°

We can also perform some basic image manipulations. Let's have a look at the Apress logo.

```
img_array = imageio.imread('apress_logo.png')

flipped_vertical = np.flipud(img_array)
flipped_horizontal = np.fliplr(img_array)
rotated_90 = np.rot90(img_array)

print("Basic manipulations completed!")
imageio.imwrite("apress_logo.png", img_array) # Fig 5.2 a)
imageio.imwrite("apress_logo_flipped_vertical.png", flipped_vertical) # Fig. 5.2. b)
imageio.imwrite("apress_logo_flipped_horizontal.png", flipped_horizontal) # Fig 5.3 a)
imageio.imwrite("apress_logo_rotated_90.png", rotated_90) # Fig 5.3 b)
```

Here are the results of the code:

Advanced Filtering

The following example requires the Fourier transform, which is not covered in this book. The Fourier transform is used to calculate the spectrum of a signal and is one of the most frequently used mathematical operations. If you don't know it, I can highly recommend learning it, even though it will probably take you quite a while to understand it.

We can also do much more advanced filtering. For example, we can do a low-pass filter, which is the basis of the image compression algorithm JPEG. This algorithm works because it removes the high-frequency components of the image, which are barely visible to the human eye. This is why JPEG is a good compression algorithm. A very similar algorithm is used for compressing MP3 audio files and also in any other form of signal processing.

 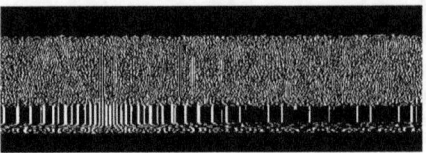

(a) The Apress logo after a low pass filter.   **(b)** The Apress logo after a high pass filter.

Fig. 5.4 The low- and high-pass filtered Apress logo

Here is some example code for the low-pass filter as seen in Figure 5.4 a):

```
import imageio
import numpy as np

img_input = imageio.imread('apress_logo.png')
img_fft = np.fft.fft2(img_input)
img_fft_filtered = img_fft * (np.abs(img_fft) > np.abs(img_fft).mean())
img_output = np.real(np.fft.ifft2(img_fft_filtered))
imageio.imwrite('apress_logo_low_pass.png', img_output.astype(np.uint8))
```

The code above takes the image, transforms it into the frequency domain, and removes the high-frequency components. Then it transforms it back into the spatial domain and writes it to a file.

We can also calculate the high-pass filter by removing the low-frequency components. The only difference is the comparison operator.

```
import imageio
import numpy as np

img_input = imageio.imread('apress_logo.png')
img_fft = np.fft.fft2(img_input)
img_fft_filtered = img_fft * (np.abs(img_fft) <= np.abs(img_fft).mean())
img_output = np.real(np.fft.ifft2(img_fft_filtered))
imageio.imwrite('apress_logo_high_pass.png', img_output.astype(np.uint8))
```

As you can see in Figure 5.4 a), applying the low-pass filter makes the image noisy, but you can still clearly see the Apress logo. When applying the high pass filter, on the other hand, you lose all the valuable information and you are only left with noise, as seen in Figure 5.4 b).

If you count the pixels of the image, it is still the same for the original and the filtered version. If you save the image pixel by pixel, it still has the same size for both versions. But here comes the kicker: you can store the image in the Fourier space where you applied the filter. Without filtering, the Fourier transform and the actual image need the same amount of space. But with filtering, the Fourier transform data is much smaller than the actual image because we discarded all the high frequency components.

In order to check that I didn't make any mistakes, we can add the low-pass and the high-pass images. This should give us the original image.

Fig. 5.5 The Apress logo after adding the low-pass and high-pass images

```
import imageio
import numpy as np

img_low_pass = imageio.imread('apress_logo_low_pass.png')
img_high_pass = imageio.imread('apress_logo_high_pass.png')
img_output = img_low_pass + img_high_pass
imageio.imwrite('apress_logo_low_pass_plus_high_pass.png', img_output.astype(np.uint8))
```

The result can be seen in Figure 5.5. As expected, it is almost identical to the original image. The only difference is rounding errors due to the Fourier transform.

Random Numbers

Random numbers have become extremely important in today's world. You can simulate many phenomena using randomly chosen numbers. This is also known as Monte Carlo simulation. This is because a gambler in Monte Carlo could not calculate a probability but wanted to determine it approximately using random numbers. Furthermore, random numbers are also irreplaceable in cryptography.

> **Random Number Algorithms**
> Random numbers are generally calculated using the formula $x_{n+1} = (a \cdot x_n + b) \mod m$. The numbers a, b, and m can be chosen according to the range of random numbers that you need, and the number x_0 is the seed. This algorithm can generate at most m different numbers; though if the combination of a, b, and m is chosen poorly, it can be much lower than that.

Here we will work with the random library from Python. You should expressly NOT use this library for cryptography, as it only returns numbers that look random, but, in reality, they are the result of a calculation. So, it is theoretically possible to draw conclusions from one number about the previous or subsequent numbers. For our purposes here, and probably almost everything you will do with random numbers, this library is good enough. For most cases it is actually a good thing if numbers are reproducible because this makes troubleshooting much easier.

The random.random() function generates uniformly distributed random numbers between 0 and 1. We also set the random seed so that the numbers obtained are reproducible.

```
>>> import random
>>> random.seed(0)
>>> random.random()
0.8444218515250481
```

We can also play around a bit with the random numbers around the seed. Make sure that every time we set the seed to 0, the next random number is 0.844..., the next after that is 0.757..., etc.

```
>>> random.random()
0.7579544029403025
>>> random.random()
```

```
0.420571580830845
>>> random.seed(0)
>>> random.random()
0.8444218515250481
```

Often, you want random numbers that are distributed differently. There are various ways to do this.

If you want random numbers that are between 0 and 2 and are evenly distributed, you can multiply the random numbers by 2. For example:

```
>>> random.seed(0)
>>> 2*random.random()
1.6888437030500962
```

You can also randomly select a number from a list.

```
>>> test_list = [1, 4, 5, 2, 7]
>>> random.seed(0)
>>> random.choice(test_list)
2
```

You often need random integer numbers that are in a certain range. You can get these with the following code:

```
>>> random.seed(0)
>>> random.randint(3,9)
9
```

It can also happen that you want to work with numbers that are not evenly distributed. Here, too, there are various ways of generating such numbers. The first option is to use the normally distributed numbers of the following function:

```
>>> random.seed(0)
>>> random.gauss(mu=0, sigma=1)
0.9417154046806644
```

The `gauss` function gives you random numbers that are Gaussian distributed. You can use `mu` to determine the center and `sigma` to determine the width of the distribution.

Calculating Pi

A very common, albeit inefficient, example of using random numbers is the calculation of Pi. The idea is to randomly select points in a square and then check how many of them are inside a circle. The ratio of the number of points inside the circle to the total number of points gives an approximation of Pi.

```
import random

n = 100000
inside_circle = 0
random.seed(0)

for _ in range(n):
    x = random.uniform(-1, 1)
    y = random.uniform(-1, 1)
    if x**2 + y**2 <= 1:
        inside_circle += 1
pi_estimate = (inside_circle / n) * 4
print(pi_estimate) # 3.129
```

Functions and Methods

Functions are ubiquitous in software development. If you see a few round brackets () in Python, it is probably a function. `split`, `enumerate`, `range`, and `append` are some functions we have already seen. Functions are operations that act on their arguments and either change them, return a new value, or have some other effect, such as opening a file.

> **Functions vs. Methods**
> Functions inside classes are also referred to as methods. So the only difference is that methods act on an instance variable of that class. Otherwise, functions and methods are almost identical. For this reason, most things that I write about functions also hold for methods. So forgive me if I use the terms interchangeably.

Take the `print` function, for example. This takes a function argument and prints its value. The `print` function is a bit special in that it does not change any values but is only there to show a value to the user.

Functions are often used for mathematical operations. The notation of a function is therefore very similar to that of mathematics. A function has a name followed by parentheses containing the arguments (a tuple). The arguments are the values the function processes. The function then often returns a value. This can be pretty much any object that can be defined in Python.

> **Length of Functions**
> Functions should be as short as possible. There's generally nothing wrong with making them as short as possible. If you want, you can write functions that are one line long. On the other hand, you should not write functions that are about 20 lines long. If functions are so long, they become extremely difficult to understand. But ultimately, it's up to you. You have to decide if a function is still easy to understand.

To define a function, you need the `def` keyword. This is followed by the name of the function, and its arguments in parentheses as well as a colon. A particularity of Python is that the contents of the function *must* be indented. This is how Python knows what belongs to the function and what doesn't. On the other hand, you don't need any curly brackets around the function body. Here is a simple example of a function that adds two numbers.

```
def add(a, b):
    return a + b
```

The `add` function takes two arguments, `a` and `b`, and returns their sum. The function can now be called as follows:

```
>>> add(3, 4)
7
```

It is important to note that the function call has the same number of arguments as the function definition. If you pass more or fewer arguments, an error is returned.

```
>>> add(3)
Traceback (most recent call last):
File "<stdin>", line 1, in <module>
TypeError: add() missing 1 required positional argument: 'b'
```

Python tells us in the error message that the required argument `b` is missing. The same applies if you pass too many function arguments.

Keyword Arguments

Keyword arguments are another way of passing function arguments. The name of the argument is connected to the value. This makes the code more readable and allows you to ignore the order of the arguments.

```
def print_name_n_times(name, n):
    for _ in range(n):
        print(name)
```

> **The Underscore _**
> It happens once in a while that you don't need a variable, but according to Python syntax, you cannot just omit it. In the for loop above, removing the _ would result in an error. In Python, it is commonly agreed that the underscore is used as a placeholder for variables that are not needed.

The common way to call this function is as follows:

```
>>> print_name_n_times("anna", 2)
anna
anna
```

But in Python, you can also use called keywords to pass the arguments. You can take the name of the function argument and assign a value to it. This way, you can pass the arguments in any order.

```
>>> print_name_n_times(name="mike", n=1)
mike
>>> print_name_n_times(n=1, name="mike")
mike
```

We can also use the keywords for just a few specific arguments. In this case, we need to pass the arguments in the correct order. If we pass arguments with keywords before arguments without keywords, Python will return an error message.

```
>>> print_name_n_times("anna", n=2)
anna
anna
>>> print_name_n_times(n=2, "anna")
File "<stdin>", line 1
SyntaxError: positional argument follows keyword argument
```

Python complains here that a positional argument (one without a keyword) follows a keyword argument. This is not allowed.

Instead of using keywords, you can also define variables with the corresponding values. The following two code examples are largely equivalent, except that with variables, you are bound to the order of the arguments.

```
>>> print_name_n_times(name="anna", n=2)
anna
anna
>>> name = "anna"
>>> n = 2
>>> print_name_n_times(name, n)
anna
anna
```

Functions generally have the problem that they become incomprehensible if they have too many arguments. This gets a little better with keywords, but it's still not ideal. We'll see in the classes topic how to solve this problem by storing multiple arguments in one object. Until then, try to use as few arguments as possible. As a rule of thumb, you should use three arguments at most. If you have more than about five arguments, you should seriously rethink your code.

> **Magic Numbers**
>
> Numbers that seem to come out of nowhere are called magic numbers. As you read the code, you see only the value of this number but no name. This is terrible, as you frequently don't understand what the number is supposed to represent. It's like magic, in a bad sense. That's why these numbers are called magic numbers.
>
> For this reason, you should *always* assign numbers to a variable with a meaningful name.

Default Arguments

Sometimes you want certain function arguments to have a default value. Unless you specify another value, the default value is used. This is very useful for hiding values that are usually the same. Here is an example of a function that calculates the power of a number. The default value for the exponent is 2.

```python
def power(x, exponent=2):
    return x**exponent
```

The function can now be called as follows:

```
>>> power(3)
9
>>> power(3, 3)
27
```

We can still use keywords, even with arguments that do not have a default value.

```
>>> power(x=3, exponent=3)
27
```

The only thing you can't do is pass arguments without a default value after arguments with a default value. This will result in an error message.

```
>>> power(exponent=3, 3)
File "<stdin>", line 1
SyntaxError: positional argument follows keyword argument
```

args and kwargs

Sometimes you want to pass an arbitrary number of arguments to a function. This is possible with the `*` and `**` operators. The `*` operator is used to pass an arbitrary number of arguments, while the `**` operator is used to pass an arbitrary number of keyword arguments. This is very useful if you don't know how many arguments you will need.

```python
def dealing_with_args(*args, **kwargs):
    for arg in args:
        print(arg)
    for key, value in kwargs.items():
        print(f"{key}: {value}")

dealing_with_args(1, 2, a=3, b=4)
# prints:
# 1
# 2
# a: 3
# b: 4
```

Though you shouldn't use `*args` as lightly as I did here. If all elements in `*args` are considered equal, you should use a list instead to make your intention clearer.

An example where you use `*args` and `**kwargs` is when you write a wrapper. A decorator is a small layer of code that you wrap around a function. You should be able to use it for any number of arguments, so you use `*args` and `**kwargs` as arguments of the decorator and pass them on to the function you are wrapping.

```python
def add(a, b):
    print(a + b)

def wrapper(*args, **kwargs):
    print("Before function call")
    add(*args, **kwargs)
    print("After function call")

wrapper(1, 2)
```

In many programming languages, `*args` are the arguments of the `main` function. In Python, this is not the case. In Python, you have to use `sys.argv` to access the command-line arguments.

A simple example looks like this:

```python
import sys

def main(argv):
    print(argv)

if __name__ == "__main__":
    main(sys.argv)
```

If you run this code with the command `python ./code.py 1 a=2`, you will get the following output:

```
python argv.py 1 a=2
['./argv.py', '1', 'a=2']
```

Command-line arguments can be useful as you don't always want to open and change your code just because you change some parameters. However, they can become confusing if you overdo it. If you have many parameters you want to set, you should use a configuration file instead.

Function Overloading

In C++, there is a concept called function overloading. You can define two functions with the same name but a different function signature, and the compiler will know which function to call.

```cpp
#include <iostream>
using namespace std;

void f(int x) {
    cout << "int" << endl;
}

void f(double x) {
    cout << "double" << endl;
}

int main() {
    f(3); // prints "int"
    f(3.0); // prints "double"
}
```

This is not possible in Python, as there is neither a compiler nor strong typing. If there are two functions with the same name, the function will simply be overwritten, even if the function signatures of these functions are different.

What you can do instead is define a function that checks the arguments for their type and then calls the appropriate function. This is not as elegant as function overloading, but it works.

```python
def f_int():
    print("int")

def f_float():
    print("float")
```

```python
def f(x):
    if type(x) == int:
        f_int()
    elif type(x) == float:
        f_float()

f(3) # prints "int"
f(3.0) # prints "float"
```

Control Flow

Functions are only executed once they are called and not in the location where they are defined. This means that in the following code, ``World'' is printed before ``Hello''.

```python
def f():
    print("Hello")

print("World")
f()
```

Now, this used to be different a long time ago. Back in the days, code was executed from top to bottom. And then you were using `goto` statements to jump to a certain location in the code. This was a very error-prone way of programming and is not used anymore. It turned out that functions and loops can do the same thing, but are much easier to understand.

So always remember: functions define a piece of code, but they are only executed when they are called.

Function Definition Order

The order in which you define your functions doesn't matter in Python. You can define the outermost function before the innermost function. This is because Python reads the whole file before executing it. This is different from C++, where you have to define a function before you can use it. For this reason, the following code works:

```python
def a():
    b()

def b():
    print("hello")

a() # Hello
```

Inside the definition of `a`, you don't know yet what the function `b` is. But this is not a problem in Python.

On the other hand, you cannot use a function call before you define a function. The following code returns an error:

```python
a() # NameError: name 'a' is not defined

def a():
    b()

def b():
    print("hello")
```

I find this behavior slightly confusing, but I can't change it. Generally, I recommend writing the functions starting with the innermost first to prevent such issues. Though it is up to you whether you follow this advice. If your code becomes unreadable because of this advice, it is high time you split your source files into many smaller files that you import.

Cyclic Dependencies

A cyclic dependency occurs if one piece of code calls the other one and vice versa. For example, if function a calls function b and function b calls function a.

```
def a():
    b()

def b():
    a()
```

I will not execute this code as it will run forever. But even if it didn't, it is still bad design. You should always avoid cyclic dependencies at all costs, be it for functions or imports. Cyclic dependencies are a sign that you haven't understood the logic of the problem you are trying to solve.

Recursion

Recursion is a concept in programming where a function calls itself. This may sound a bit strange at first, but it is a very powerful concept. There are some problems that you can easily solve by using recursion. The most common ones are tree algorithms (p. 64).

Recursion is a common method to calculate the factorial of a number.

```
def factorial(n):
    if n == 0:
        return 1
    return n * factorial(n-1)

print(factorial(5)) # 120
```

Here you can see the basic functionality of recursion. You have a function `factorial` that calls itself. Only if the counter reaches 0 do you return some value.

Of course, it is also possible to write code without recursion that calculates the factorial of a number. Just because there exists a recursive solution doesn't mean that it is always the best one.

```
def factorial(n):
    result = 1
    for i in range(1, n+1):
        result *= i
    return result

print(factorial(5)) # 120
```

I think that in this case, it is up to you to decide which code you prefer.

Fig. 6.1 The graphical representation of a very small tree

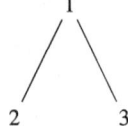

A more elaborate example of a recursive problem is as follows: you have different coins, and you want to know how many ways you can combine them to get a certain amount. Here is the code for this problem:

```
coins_available = [10, 5, 2, 1]
def get_coins(amount, coins_used, max_value):
    if amount == 0:
        print(coins_used)
    for coin_value in coins_available:
        if coin_value <= amount and coin_value <= max_value:
            get_coins(amount-coin_value,
                      coins_used+[coin_value],
                      coin_value)

get_coins(amount=15,
          coins_used=[],
          max_value=coins_available[0])
# prints [10, 5], and many more values
```

Here the function `get_coins` calls itself recursively. Only if the `amount` is 0 does the recursion stop and print the coins accumulated.

Note that I had to use integer values for the coins. When using floating point values, on the other hand, for example `0.2`, you have to be very careful with the `==` and `<=` operators, as there will be rounding errors due to the finite precision of floating point numbers. This problem is not limited to Python, but occurs in all programming languages.

Trees

Trees are not a built-in data structure in Python. However, they can be extremely useful, as there are many algorithms that run on trees quite efficiently.

If you ever encounter a problem with a recursive data structure, you should use a tree. A tree consists of nodes, which contain other nodes, also known as children. The first node is called the root node, and nodes that don't contain any other nodes are called leaf nodes. In our example in Figure 6.1, the root of our tree is the node 1, while 2 and 3 are leafs.

Here is an example of how one can implement a tree in Python. In Python, this is pretty simple. We also add a value to all nodes. This is not necessary; you could also define a tree that stores its information otherwise. For example, if the tree contains nodes of different types.

```
class Node:
    def __init__(self, value):
        self.value = value
        self.children = []
```

```python
    def add_child(self, child):
        self.children.append(child)

root = Node(1)
child1 = Node(2)
root.add_child(child1)
child2 = Node(3)
root.add_child(child2)
```

The sum of all values in this tree can be calculated as follows. Note that we always use recursion when working with trees. We call the same function on all children of the node.

```python
def sum_tree(node):
    sum = node.value
    for child in node.children:
        sum += sum_tree(child)
    return sum

print(sum_tree(root)) # 6
```

Classes 7

As I already mentioned, you should only store objects with the same properties in lists, even though you can store anything you want there in Python. However, the code becomes unreadable if you do this. To store different properties of an object, you should define a class. To do this, we start with data classes, which are intended to store data and no methods. Though you can do pretty much everything you want in Python, you can also create data classes containing methods (functions inside a class).

```
from dataclasses import dataclass

@dataclass
class Address:
    name: str
    street: str
    city: str
```

Here we have also introduced type hints with the `: str` notation. These tell the user what values should be used for a specific variable. However, unlike C++, in Python, these type hints are not enforced. You can pass any object you want; it just might not work.

Now we have defined a structured object that can store a person's entire address at once. As we defined a dataclass, there is already a constructor that initializes the object. This allows us to write the following code:

```
my_address = Address(name="Donald Duck",
                    street="1847 Bungalow Lane",
                    city="Duckburg")
print(my_address)
# Address(name='Donald Duck', street='1847 Bungalow Lane',
#   city='Duckburg')
print(my_address.name) # Donald Duck
```

This is extremely useful. We no longer have to "carry around" this information, such as the street and the town, separately, but we can store them together in an address. We can therefore significantly reduce the mental strain. We only need a single word to store three things at once. If you are not yet convinced of the usefulness of such objects, imagine a car. How many individual parts does a car consist of? And do you have any idea what they all do? Probably not. But you are nevertheless very familiar with the concept of a car. And when you get into a new car, you know exactly how to operate it.

> **Classes vs. Lists**
>
> Now we have seen two constructs that allow us to store multiple objects together: lists and classes. Now the question is: what are the differences?
>
> Let's look at some example code:
>
> ```python
> class Address:
>     def __init__(self, name, street, city):
>         self.name = name
>         self.street = street
>         self.city = city
>
> my_address = Address("Donald Duck",
>                     "1847 Bungalow Lane",
>                     "Duckburg")
> print(my_address.name) # Donald Duck
>
> my_other_address = ["Mickey Mouse",
>                     "123 Main Street",
>                     "Disneyland"]
> print(my_other_address[0]) # Mickey Mouse
> ```
>
> Now the question is: which code is better?
>
> In order to judge this question, we always have to look at the user code first.
>
> ```python
> print(my_address.name) # Donald Duck
> print(my_other_address[0]) # Mickey Mouse
> ```
>
> If you read this code a few times, you will probably notice that the first line is much more readable than the second because you don't know what element [0] returns. This means that the first line is better. Period. Using classes to store structured objects is strictly better than using lists.

The ability to store different objects together has been around for a long time. The C programming language, which appeared in 1972, already allowed different objects to be stored together using so-called "structs." However, C was not yet "object-oriented" (OO), whatever that term means exactly. The extension to use classes only came with C++ and other programming languages. With C++, programs got the opportunity to store functions alongside variables in classes in a convenient way. Functions within classes are also called methods. These methods can always access all other methods, as well as all variables within the class. Classes can therefore be used to bundle a piece of code in a very practical way.

The ability to store functions in a "struct" was already available with C. C even allowed you to hide things from the user by simply omitting them in the header file. The private keyword in C++ only had to be introduced because the compiler needs to know all the members of a class, and therefore, they have to be listed in the header files. However, using functions in structs was very tedious and error-prone. With classes, this became much easier.

As a summary, one can say that classes did not bring any fundamentally new concepts to programming. They only made it easier to use the existing concepts. If you don't like classes, you can also write code using only data classes (or structs if you program in C or C++) and functions.

Now you may be wondering why you should hide something from a user. Perhaps the user wants to know all the details of your code?

This is indeed a very important question. But again, let's have a look at a car. Do you really want to know the meaning of every single part, or do you just want to drive it around? Sure, there are nerds who can take a car apart and put it back together again by themselves, but that is the absolute exception. Most "normal" people don't even change the oil themselves but leave that to the garage. Most "normal" people don't even want to know how the car works exactly because it's far too complicated. They are happy if they can drive from A to B, and they don't want to know anything else.

In code, it is similar. This is called encapsulation. Encapsulate your code as much as possible. Hide everything that can be hidden. The users of your code probably don't want to know about all the details of your code, just like you don't know what sorting algorithm Python uses by default. You don't care about this; it works, and you don't have to worry about it.

> **Single Responsibility Principle**
> One of the most important rules of thumb in software engineering is the Single Responsibility Principle (SRP). It states that any object (class, function, etc.) should do only one thing. Obeying the SRP helps you understand your code better and find appropriate names.
>
> It is hard to define what a "single responsibility" is exactly. However, you should keep this rule in mind if you work with classes. If a class is too long, it probably does several different things and should be split.

Most object-oriented programming languages have introduced the `private` attribute in order to encapsulate the code. It prevents anyone from outside the class from accessing the corresponding objects. In Python, however, this does not exist. In Python, variable names starting with one underscore _ mean by convention that this variable or function should not be used outside the class. You can ignore this convention if you want and still use it; it's just highly discouraged. That's like tinkering with the engine of a car. This is not recommended, and you do it at your own risk.

Classes and Objects

You can think of a class as a general structure given by the variables and methods, whereas an object is a specific implementation of this structure. There may be as many objects for a specific class as you want. Though generally, for every class there should be at least one object. It doesn't make much sense to have a class without any objects. That would be like designing a car without ever building one.

Here is an example of a class and an object. The class is called `Person`, and the object is called `anna`.

```
# This is the class definition
class Person:
    def __init__(self, name):
        self.name = name

# anna is an object of type Person
anna = Person("Anna")
print(anna.name) # Anna
```

There are also classes that don't have any objects. One example of such classes is abstract classes. They are used to define a common interface for multiple classes. An abstract class cannot be instantiated, but it can be inherited from. This is useful if you want to define a common interface for multiple classes without implementing it.

Another type of class that doesn't have any objects is a static class. A static class is a class that only contains static methods. These methods can be called without creating an object of the class. Here is an example of a static class:

```python
class Elements(object):
    element_list = []

    @staticmethod
    def add_element(x):
        Elements.element_list.append(x)

Elements.add_element('earth')
Elements.add_element('water')
print(Elements.element_list) # ['earth', 'water']
```

I just showed this example for the sake of completeness. Generally, I advise against using static classes. Just use a few functions instead.

Special Methods

In Python, objects come along with some special methods. The following code shows some of them:

```python
>>> [method_name for method_name in dir(object)
...               if callable(getattr(object, method_name))]
['__class__', '__delattr__', '__dir__', '__eq__', ...]
```

These methods can all be overridden if you want. The most important special methods are as follows:

- `__init__` is the constructor of an object. It is called when an object is created. This is a very important function, but you shouldn't implement any complex logic in it!
- `__str__` is called when the object is converted to a string. The goal of `__str__` is to return a readable string.
- `__repr__` is similar to `__str__`, but rather than readability, the goal is to return an unambiguous string.
- `__eq__` defines the behavior of the `==` operator. It should return `True` if the two objects are equal and `False` otherwise.
- `__dict__` returns the dictionary of the object. This is useful if you want to see all the attributes of an object.

Here is a class that implements some of these special methods:

```python
class Address:
    def __init__(self, name, street, city):
        self.name = name
        self.street = street
        self.city = city

    def __str__(self):
        return f"{self.name}, {self.street}, {self.city}"

    def __eq__(self, other):
```

```
            return self.name == other.name and \
                self.street == other.street and \
                self.city == other.city

my_address = Address("Donald Duck",
                    "1847 Bungalow Lane",
                    "Duckburg")

other_adress = Address("Mickey Mouse",
                       "123 Main Street",
                       "Disneyland")

print(my_address) # Donald Duck, 1847 Bungalow Lane, Duckburg
print(my_address == other_adress) # False
print(my_address.__dict__)
# {'name': 'Donald Duck', 'street': '1847 Bungalow Lane', 'city': 'Duckburg'}
```

In Python, every object has a `__str__` method and can therefore be printed. If you convert the object into a string by using an f-string or a `print` statement, this method is called. For classes (p. 67), you can overwrite this method and define how the object should be converted into a string.

```
class Person:
    def __init__(self, name):
        self.name = name

    def __str__(self):
        return f"Dear {self.name}"

person = Person("Donald Duck")
print(person) # Dear Donald Duck
```

Special methods are generally not needed. I only use the `__init__` function on a regular basis. All other special functions are nice gimmicks. Use them if they make your code more readable.

Example

Classes are an important concept in programming, yet they are not that easy to understand at first. For this reason, I will provide an example of a simple class. It's a person who has some savings. The person can deposit and withdraw money. The person can also check how much money they have.

```
class Person:
    def __init__(self, initial_savings, hourly_wage):
        self._amount_saved = initial_savings
        self._hourly_wage = hourly_wage

    def deposit(self, amount):
        self._amount_saved += amount

    def withdraw(self, amount):
        self._amount_saved -= amount

    def work(self, hours):
        self._amount_saved += hours * self._hourly_wage

    def read_balance_sheet(self):
        return self._amount_saved
```

This example is very similar to reality, which is a good sign. Probably, we got the code right. In reality, you are not able to control the `amount_saved` variable directly. You can only deposit and withdraw money, or you can go to work. This is exactly what we have implemented here. The `deposit`, `withdraw`, and `work` functions are the only ways to change the amount of money you own.

The code using this class could look something like this:

```
anna = Person(initial_savings=100, hourly_rate=10)
anna.deposit(100)
anna.work(10)
anna.withdraw(50)
print(anna.read_balance_sheet()) # 250
```

Now we can refine this class further. With the code in its current form, it would be easy for the `amount_saved` to become negative. There are several possibilities that the balance can become negative. The most obvious one is that the person withdraws more money than they have. Another possibility is that the person deposits a negative amount to their bank account. This is less exotic than it sounds. In fact, such tricks were the origin of hacking.

```
thief = Person(0, 0)
print(thief.read_balance_sheet()) # 0
thief.deposit(-100)
print(thief.read_speed_from()) # -100
```

We want to prevent this behavior. The balance may never be negative.

There are several ways the balance may become negative. We will only look at two cases:

- The person deposits a negative amount.
- The person withdraws more money than he owns.

Another question is how the code should deal with these two cases. Answering such questions is frequently more difficult than implementing the corresponding code. The following assumptions seem reasonable to me:

- If the person deposits a negative amount, we raise an exception because the person is not allowed to do this.
- If the person withdraws more money than they have, we give them all the money and set the balance to 0.

> **Requirements Engineering**
> What the code should do is by no means obvious. It happens very often that the software team develops a piece of software that is not used at all. This is because the software does not meet the requirements of the user. For this reason, it is very important to have some requirements engineers in the team who are in constant contact with the potential users. A famous case of failed requirements engineering (though it was not in software development) was Nokia, who didn't see the potential of the smartphone, even though some of its engineers suggested developing a phone without a keyboard.

```
class Person:
    # ...

    def deposit(self, amount):
        if amount < 0:
            raise ValueError("You can't deposit a negative amount.")
        self._amount_saved += amount

    def withdraw(self, amount):
        if amount > self._amount_saved:
            self._amount_saved = 0
        else:
            self._amount_saved -= amount

    # ...
```

Now we can create different people with different savings and hourly wages:

```
student = Person(initial_savings=10, hourly_wage=10)
lawyer = Person(initial_savings=1000, hourly_wage=100)
```

Classes are an enormously helpful construct. You store the variables and the functions together; it's easy to write the code, and everything is fine. Isn't it? Well, not quite. If only programming were that easy... Unfortunately, classes also have their own set of disadvantages. Otherwise, there wouldn't be groups of programmers who like to program functionally. The Linux kernel is written in C, which also doesn't have classes. If classes were so great, why would you use anything else?

> **Global Variables and Member Variables**
> One of the worst things in software development is global variables. You define them at the beginning of your code, and you can use them everywhere. This sounds amazing, but this is among the worst habits in programming.
>
> With normal variables that you pass as function arguments, you know quite exactly where they are used and what value they have. With global variables, on the other hand, you have no idea. They could be changed anywhere in the code. This is an absolute nightmare. Global variables can be altered anywhere in the code, and you have no idea where they are changed. This is a nightmare for debugging. You can never be sure what the value of a global variable is at any time. This is why you should avoid global variables at all costs.
>
> A similar problem exists with member variables of a class. They can be used anywhere within the class, and if the class is huge, you'll face a similar problem as with global variables. For this reason, it is paramount that you keep your classes small!

Code has the tendency to grow, and the same holds true for classes. It's just too convenient to add another method to a class. After all, it gives you access to all the private variables. This creates the temptation to make classes as large as possible. However, this also makes them extremely complicated and difficult to understand. The size at which you can no longer understand a class is much lower than you would expect. Already, a 50-line-long class can be an absolute nightmare if it's badly written. The problem is that the class variables store states that are changed and used by the functions. This quickly leads to a high degree of complexity that you can no longer comprehend. The only solution is to break the class into small pieces. But once you've reached the point where you no longer understand the class, you can't break it down into smaller pieces. So, you have an even bigger problem.

The solution is to keep classes small. It's hard to say exactly how big "small" is, but it's certainly smaller than most classes I encountered in the wild. Classes should certainly be shorter than 100 lines. A good rule of thumb is that the size of a class is still acceptable as long as you can write tests (p. 91) for the class. Because in order to write tests, you also have to understand what the class does exactly. If you can write tests for a class, it can't be so complicated that it's really problematic.

One of the strengths of classes is the fact that we can store different objects, in this case, persons, in the same list. Let's take our two people that we've already created and create a list with them.

```
student = Person(initial_savings=10, hourly_wage=10)
lawyer = Person(initial_savings=1000, hourly_wage=100)
people = [student, lawyer]
```

Now we can call the `withdraw_money` function for all people at the same time.

```
for person in people:
    person.withdraw_money(100)

for person in people:
    print(person.read_balance()) # 0, 900
```

`student` and `lawyer` are both of the type `Person`. These objects could already be stored in the same list in C++ since they are both instances of the same class.

But Python can do much more. Python supports so-called "duck typing." If it quacks like a duck and looks like a duck, then it is a duck. In terms of code, this means that Python supports all types for our code that have implemented the required methods. As Python only checks at runtime if the required methods are implemented, we can now also implement a class `Billionaire`, which has an infinite amount of money, and the only thing a billionaire can do is to withdraw money. This class looks something like this:

```
class Billionaire:
    def withdraw(self, amount):
        pass

    def read_balance_sheet(self):
        return "Billions"
```

Now we can create instances of `Person` and `Billionaire` and store them in the same list. In C++, this would not be possible because these are different types with different interfaces.

Afterwards, we can also call the `withdraw` function for all objects in the list and read out the balance sheet. However, we are not allowed to call `work` for all the people in our list, as this function is not implemented for the `Billionaire` class.

```
student = Person(initial_savings=10, hourly_wage=10)
lawyer = Person(initial_savings=1000, hourly_wage=100)
BillGates = Billionaire()
people = [student, lawyer, BillGates]

for person in people:
    person.withdraw(100)
```

This duck typing has its advantages, but also its drawbacks. In C++, the compiler will tell you if some code cannot be executed because a function is not implemented. In Python, on the other hand, you might run your code, but in the middle of the execution, it fails because it tries to access a function that doesn't exist. Duck typing is a double-edged sword.

Let's see what happens if the `Billionaire` tries to work.

```
BillGates = Billionaire()
BillGates.work()
# Traceback (most recent call last):
# File "<stdin>", line 1, in <module>
# AttributeError: 'Billionaire' object has no attribute 'work'
```

Python wants to tell us that the method `work` is not implemented for the class `Billionaire`. What we do with this message is our problem. For example, we can implement an empty function `work` for the `Billionaire`. Or we can make sure that `work` is never called for any billionaire.

```
class Billionaire:
# ...
    def work(self, hours):
        pass
# ...
```

This solves the problem, and we will no longer receive error messages. Conversely, it can be confusing that the `Billionaire` now implements the `work` function but cannot work. Perhaps it is better if the `work` function effectively returns an error for the `Billionaire`.

I hope you can see that in software development, there are often many options, but it is not clear which one to choose. It all depends on what exactly you want to achieve with the code. And what you want to achieve is not that easy to determine. Finding out exactly what the code should be able to do is often more effort than implementing the code!

Inheritance

Inheritance is a concept in object-oriented programming. It allows a class to take over functionality from another class. The class "inherits" the methods and variables of the parent class. This may seem very useful at first glance, as it saves you a lot of repetitive code. However, it is also very dangerous, as it strongly couples the code. Changes in the parent class affect the child class, and sometimes even the other way around. This can lead to very complex and difficult-to-understand code. For this reason, inheritance should only be used very sparingly.

It must be said that a distinction is made between two different types of inheritance. The first type is the one we have already discussed. A class inherits all the functionality of another class. This is called "implementation inheritance." The other type is "interface inheritance," where a class inherits only the interface of another class, but no functionality. This type of inheritance is much less problematic because it doesn't couple the classes. Furthermore, interfaces are much more stable than implementations and change less frequently.

Implementation Inheritance

Here is an example of implementation inheritance. The classes `Mountainbike` and `Roadbike` inherit from the class `Bicycle`. This means that we can instantiate an object of the class `Mountainbike` and use it to call the function `number_of_gears` of the parent class.

```
class Bicycle:
    def number_of_gears(self):
        print(f"Has 12 gears")
```

```python
class Mountainbike(Bicycle):
    pass

class Roadbike(Bicycle):
    def number_of_gears(self):
        print(f"Has 2 times 11 gears")

my_mountainbike = Mountainbike()
my_mountainbike.number_of_gears() # Has 12 gears
my_roadbike = Roadbike()
my_roadbike.number_of_gears() # Has 2 times 11 gears
```

However, the principle applies: "Prefer composition over inheritance." With composition, the same functionality can be achieved with just a little more code, but with significantly less coupling. And this little bit of extra code is worth it as it makes the code more readable.

```python
class OneByGear:
    def get_number_of_gears(self):
        print(f"Has 12 gears")

class TwoByGear:
    def get_number_of_gears(self):
        print(f"Has 2 times 11 gears")

class Montainbike():
    self.gear = OneByGear()

    def get_numer_of_gears(self):
        self.gear.get_number_of_gears()

class Roadbike():
    self.gear = TwoByGear()

    def get_number_of_gears(self):
        self.gear.get_number_of_gears()

my_mountainbike = Mountainbike()
my_mountainbike.get_number_of_gears() # Has 12 gears
my_roadbike = Roadbike()
my_roadbike.get_number_of_gears() # Has 2 times 11 gears
```

The only drawback of composition I see is that naming can be a little bit more difficult when writing the code. With inheritance, it is "clear" that the `Roadbike` is a `Bicycle` and therefore inherits from it. With composition, you have to come up with a name for the variable that stores the `Gear` object. But this is a small price to pay for the advantages of composition.

> **Prefer Composition over Inheritance**
> It may not be apparent to you yet, but you shouldn't use implementation inheritance. Just like global variables, implementation inheritance seems like a great thing. After all, it allows you to reuse code. But after using it for a while, you'll realize its drawbacks. The main issue is that it couples the classes very strongly. You will have a really hard time refactoring the code if there is inheritance everywhere. Furthermore, you'll never know where a function is actually implemented. And maybe you found a definition, but it is overridden somewhere.
>
> When using composition, you always know where some functionality is defined as you call it from the corresponding object. This is a little bit more code, but it makes it much clearer.

There is the old rule saying that a `Roadbike` is a `Bike` and therefore the `Roadbike` should inherit from the `Bike` class. This is a very old dogma that is still being taught in many places, but it is wrong. You should only implement something if it makes sense from an implementation point of view, and if there is no common functionality, `Roadbike` should certainly not inherit from `Bike`. This is besides the fact that I generally don't recommend using inheritance.

Interface Inheritance

Interface inheritance is much less problematic than implementation inheritance. With interface inheritance, only the interface of a class is inherited, not the functionality (i.e., no implemented methods or variables). The inheriting classes must implement this interface accordingly by defining the functions and variables themselves.

In Python, a class can inherit from the class `ABC` to define an abstract base class (an interface, as they would call it in Java). A class that inherits from such a base class *must* implement all the functions of the interface that are decorated with the `@abstractmethod` decorator. If a class does not implement all the functions, an error message is displayed. In the following example, the function `area` is an `@abstractmethod` and is not implemented in the base class. It must be implemented accordingly by all classes that inherit from `Shape`.

```python
from abc import ABC, abstractmethod

class Shape(ABC):
    @abstractmethod
    def area(self):
        pass

class Rectangle(Shape):
    def __init__(self, a, b):
        self.a = a
        self.b = b

    def area(self):
        return self.a * self.b

my_square = Rectangle(3, 3)
print(my_square.area()) # 9
```

If you write the function name `area` incorrectly in the class `Rectangle`, you get an error message. This is in contrast to implementation inheritance, where there is no error message, but the function of the parent class is simply called instead. The code with implementation inheritance is extremely brittle, and brittle code is bad.

```python
class Circle(Shape):
    def __init__(self, r):
        self.r = r

    def areaaa(self):
        return 3.14*self.r**2

my_circle = Circle(2)
# TypeError: Can't instantiate abstract class
# Circle with abstract method area
```

This code already returns an error message if you instantiate a `Circle` object. You don't even get to call the `area` function. This is a good thing as the code should return an error as early as possible.

> **When to Use Abstract Base Classes**
>
> There is no need to use abstract base classes if you don't want to. Contrary to C++, you don't need base classes to implement polymorphism. In Python, using abstract base classes is a purely cosmetic choice.
>
> It is hard to tell when base classes in Python are really useful. One example is if you have a student who has to implement a set of classes. You can define an abstract base class with these functions, and the student has to implement them. Or it might be useful if you want to define a public interface.

Encapsulation

When designing a class, it is of utmost importance to encapsulate the code as much as possible. This means that you should hide all the details of the implementation from the user. The user should have only a very small interface to the class. Generally, this interface consists of a few functions that the user can call. All the variables and some of the functions are hidden from the user. This is the idea of encapsulation.

If you don't understand the idea of encapsulation, think of a car. You can drive it, but you don't know how it works. You don't know how the engine works, how the brakes work, or how the steering works. You just drive it. This is exactly what encapsulation is about. The user of your code should not have to know how it works internally. He should just use it.

In Python, it's not possible to hide variables from the user. You can't make a variable private. It's just a convention that variables and methods that start with an underscore are not to be used by the user. Unlike other languages, this is just a convention, and it is not enforced by the language. It is highly discouraged to use variables that start with an underscore. Use the interface that you are supposed to use. Accessing private variables is like peeking under the hood of a car. It is not a good idea.

Here is a class with private variables:

```python
class Car:
    def __init__(self):
        self._speed = 0

    def accelerate(self, amount):
        self._speed += amount

    def decelerate(self, amount):
        self._speed -= amount

    def get_speed(self):
        return self._speed

my_car = Car()
my_car.accelerate(10)
print(my_car.get_speed()) # 10
```

In this example, the `_speed` variable is not to be used by the user. It is only used by the class itself. The user should only use the functions `accelerate`, `decelerate`, and `get_speed`. This is the idea of encapsulation.

> **Getters and Setters**
>
> In some programming languages, most notably Java, it is common to use getters and setters to access the variables of a class. A getter is a function that returns the value of a variable, and a setter is a function that sets the value of a variable. I think this is an antipattern and should be avoided. Let me briefly explain:
>
> Either you have a dataclass with only variables and no functions. Adding getters and setters won't help you with anything. You can still access the variables directly.
>
> Or you have a class with functions. The variables are used inside the functions. There is no need to access these variables, neither directly nor through getters and setters.
>
> Long story short: Don't write getters or setters.

Abstraction

Abstraction is the idea of hiding the complexity of a class from the user. For example, it shouldn't matter what type of engine you have in your car. There might be minor differences like the acceleration or the range, but the car should drive the same way no matter if it has an electric or a combustion engine. This allows you to drive any car without having to know how it works.

In programming, it is very similar. You always have to think how a common interface could look like. For example, the user of a website wants to pay either with PayPal or with their credit card. The website should not depend on this difference. It should just have to call the payment function which then handles the payment.

In programming, it happens frequently that the user and the programmer of a certain piece of code want to work with different data models. Thus, it's a common question if the user or the programmer should write the adapter code. And the answer is very clear: the programmer should write the adapter code. This is because there is usually only one programmer (or team of programmers) but multiple users. Thus, a few programmers can make the life of many users easier. This is generally worth it.

Python Modules and Packages

Modules and Imports

In Python, a module is a folder or file that contains Python code. Typically, a module contains code for a specific functionality. One example is the `math` module, which contains functions for mathematical operations. Modules can be imported into another file using the `import` statement which is one of the most common operations in Python.

Since Python 3.3, there are two types of packages: the newer namespace packages and the older regular packages. Though newer doesn't mean better. It's just a different way of creating packages. As long as you write only small packages, the difference is negligible.

There are three possibilities to create a package:

- Regular packages with import statements in the `__init__.py` file
- Regular packages with an empty `__init__.py` file
- Namespace packages

Which kind of package you create is up to you. Probably a regular package with an empty `__init__.py` file is the best choice, but it depends on what you want to achieve. What matters in the end is that the code is easy to read and maintain. And in most cases, the differences between the three options are minimal. If you don't write large libraries, you most likely don't want to bother with such details now. You may want to skip this section and come back later on.

Regular Packages

In a regular package, all files are stored in a directory. Furthermore, it has to contain a file called `__init__.py`. This file can be empty, but it has to exist. The `__init__.py` file is used to initialize the package. It contains code that is executed when the package is imported. In theory, it can contain any code you could think of, but it is most common to use it to define the public interface of the package by listing the functions and classes that are to be used by the user.

The folder structure of a regular package is as follows:

```
my_package/
    __init__.py
    math_utils.py
    string_utils.py
main.py
```

For the sake of simplicity, we assume that the `math_utils.py` and `string_utils.py` files only contain the functions that are to be used by the user.

```python
# inside my_package/math_utils.py
def add(a, b):
    print(a + b)

# inside my_package/string_utils.py
def get_first_character(s):
    print(s[0])
```

The `my_package/__init__.py` file can look like this:

```python
# inside my_package/__init__.py
from .math_utils import add
from .string_utils import get_first_character
```

You can now import the functions from the package in another file using the following code:

```python
import my_package

my_package.add(1, 2) # Output: 3
my_package.get_first_character("Hello") # Output: "H"
```

Alternatively, you can import the functions directly from the package:

```python
from my_package import add, get_first_character

add(1, 2)                    # Output: 3
get_first_character("Hello") # Output: "H"
```

If the `my_package/__init__.py` file is empty, you can import the functions directly from the package; however, the code becomes slightly more verbose.

```python
from my_package.math_utils import add
from my_package.string_utils import get_first_character

add(1, 2)                    # Output: 3
get_first_character("Hello") # Output: "H"
```

Namespace Packages

A namespace package can be split up into multiple files that all have the same name, but are located in different folders.

Let's say we have the following folder structure:

```
my_project/
    math/utils/math_utils.py
    string/utils/string_utils.py
main.py
```

And the code of the modules is as follows:

```
# inside my_project/math/utils/math_utils.py
def add(a, b):
    print(a + b)

# inside my_project/string/utils/string_utils.py
def get_first_character(s):
    print(s[0])
```

Then you can import the functions from the namespace package in the following way:

```
import sys

# Add both package parts to the path
sys.path.extend([
    '/my_project/string',
    '/my_project/math',
])

from utils import math_utils
from utils import string_utils

math_utils.add(2, 3)                          # Output: 5
string_utils.get_first_character("hello")     # Output: h
```

"Now, what's the point?" you may ask. Well, the point is that you can have multiple packages with the same name, but different contents. This is useful if you want to have different versions of a package or if you want to have different packages with the same name. Just swap the path and you're done. Furthermore, you can split up a package into multiple folders, which can be useful if you have a lot of code. You just have to call the leaf folder the same way and the user won't be able to tell the difference.

Installing Packages with Pip

It happens frequently that you have to get a package from the internet. This is where pip comes in. Pip is the package manager for Python and is installed by default when you install Python. You have to open the command line and run `pip install numpy` to install the NumPy library, for example.

If you run some code that uses NumPy without having NumPy installed, you'll get an error message:

```
Traceback (most recent call last):
    File "/home/marco/python made easy/use_numpy.py", line 1, in <module>
        import numpy
ModuleNotFoundError: No module named 'numpy'
```

As always when you encounter an error message, ask your favorite AI tool for help. It will quite certainly be able to tell you which package you have to install.

The Virtual Environment

A virtual environment is a self-contained directory that contains a Python installation for a particular version of Python, plus a number of additional packages. You can create a virtual environment (short "venv") with the following command:

```
$ python -m venv venv
```

If you are in the folder containing the venv folder, you can activate the virtual environment with the following command:

```
$ source venv/bin/activate  # in Linux
$ venv\Scripts\activate     # in Windows
```

Once you are in an active venv, you'll see the additional text "(venv)" in the command line.

```
(venv) marco@notebook:~/python made easy/code$
```

If you are in the folder containing the venv folder, you can deactivate the virtual environment with the following command:

```
$ deactivate
```

Virtual environments are very helpful in order to keep the packages used in different projects separate. This is especially important if your projects need different versions of the same package. Without pip, you would run into serious problems if you try to install different versions of the same package.

Now, of course, installing all packages will take a lot of space on your computer. But unless you have many projects, this generally isn't a problem. Especially for projects that you don't use often, you can simply delete the virtual environment and create a new one when you need it again. Use a requirements.txt file to keep track of the packages you need for your project. Then you can install them all at once with

```
pip install -r requirements.txt
```

If you ever happen to work on a project that hasn't a requirements.txt file, but you have already installed all the packages, you can create the requirements.txt file with

```
pip freeze > requirements.txt
```

If it's likely that you won't need the venv again, you can delete it by deleting the containing folder. All the venv data is stored in this folder, so deleting it will delete the venv completely.

```
rm -rf venv
```

Util 9

In this chapter, we explain some useful functionality of Python, namely, how to deal with files and time.

Files

Files are important in programming to store data. There are all kinds of possible file formats for different purposes. The most common file format is the text file. This could be anything, for example, the .tex file that I'm writing this book on, or your Python code.

CSV

But there are also a lot of files for storing structured data. A very common file format is the CSV (Comma-Separated Values) file. CSV is quite simple and can be read by any text editor and even by Microsoft Excel. The CSV file format is very simple. Each line is a row, and the columns are separated by a comma. Here is an example of a CSV file:

```
#name,age,city
Donald Duck,42,Duckburg
Mickey Mouse,40,Disneyland
```

However, CSV files also have their drawbacks. The main drawback is that there is no real standard for how they should be structured. For example, you have to know if the first line of a file is a comment or part of the data. This may seem like a minor issue to you, but I can promise that it will give you headaches if you have to deal with all kinds of different CSV files.

But there are also other issues. For example, if there are commas as part of the values, the file will be interpreted incorrectly. For this reason, it is common to use the ; character to separate the values rather than a comma.

The data from the CSV file above can be read with the following code:

```
with open("people.csv") as file:
    for row in file:
        if row.startswith("#"):
            continue
        print(row.strip().split(","))
```

Writing a CSV file is straightforward. You just have to write the values separated by a comma. Here is an example—the "w" means that we want to write a new file:

```
with open("people.csv", "w") as file:
    file.write("#name,age,city\n")
    file.write("Donald Duck,42,Duckburg\n")
    file.write("Mickey Mouse,40,Disneyland\n")
```

> **With Open**
>
> The classical way to read out the contents of a file was as follows:
>
> ```
> file = open("people.csv")
> for row in file:
>     print(row)
> file.close()
> ```
>
> If you forget to close the file, bad things could happen. What exactly happens depends on many factors. However, the fact that you can make such mistakes is a sign of bad design. In order to fix this issue, the `with open` statement was introduced. This statement automatically closes the file after the block is executed. This is a much better design.
>
> ```
> with open("people.csv") as file:
>     for row in file:
>         print(row)
> # here the file closes automatically
> ```
>
> Note that the `with` statement can also be used with other objects that support the context manager protocol.

JSON and Co

There are many file standards to store structured data. The most common ones are JSON and XML. Though the explanations given here are valid for all these file formats.

JSON may not be quite as intuitive as CSV, but it has several advantages. If you have to deal with a JSON file, you know exactly what to expect. While CSV may be good enough for flat data, JSON can also be used to store structured data. Here is an example of a JSON file:

```
{
    "people": [
        {
            "name": "Donald Duck",
            "age": 42,
            "city": "Duckburg"
        },
        {
            "name": "Mickey Mouse",
            "age": 40,
            "city": "Disneyland"
        }
    ]
}
```

Now this file is apparently much more verbose than a CSV file. But if you read the file using Python, this is not an issue. In fact, reading a JSON file is even simpler than reading a CSV file. You load it with the `json.load()` command, and then you can access the different elements with `[]`.

Here is an example code of how to read our JSON file:

```
import json

with open(people.json') as f:
    d = json.load(f)
    print(d["people"][1]["age"]) # prints 40
```

HDF5

HDF5 is a binary file format. This has the advantage that the files containing a lot of data are much smaller than text-based files. This is due to the fact that saving a floating point number takes only 8 bytes of memory, while saving it in text form may take much more than that.

Furthermore, writing and reading files is much faster. Generally, writing or reading large files is limited by the speed of your SSD. It is recommended to use HDF5 for large files.

Just like JSON, HDF5 is a structured file format. You can store data in groups, datasets, and auxiliary data. Here is an example of how to write an HDF5 file:

```
import h5py

with h5py.File('people.h5', 'w') as f:
    people = f.create_group('people')
    person1 = people.create_group('person1')
    person1.create_dataset('name', data='Donald Duck')
    person1.create_dataset('age', data=42)
    person1.create_dataset('city', data='Duckburg')
    person2 = people.create_group('person2')
    person2.create_dataset('name', data='Mickey Mouse')
    person2.create_dataset('age', data=40)
    person2.create_dataset('city', data='Disneyland')
```

Now I cannot show you the content of this file as it's in a binary format. If you want to inspect an HDF5 file, you have to download the free HDFView software.[1]

But what we can do instead is inspect the file with Python. Here is an example of how to read the file:

```
import h5py

with h5py.File('people.h5', 'r') as f:
    print(f['people']['person1']['age'][()]) # prints 42
```

SQL

SQL stands for Structured Query Language. It is the most common type of database technology. And as the name already says, it is great for making queries on petabyte-sized datasets. Usually, companies have one or more databases to store all their business data.

---

[1] https://www.hdfgroup.org/download-hdfview/

There are different accents of SQL. The most common ones are MySQL, PostgreSQL, and SQLite. SQLite is a very lightweight database that is often used for small projects. MySQL and PostgreSQL are used for larger projects.

Here we look only at SQLite as this is the easiest to use. SQLite is a database that is stored in a single file and can be created on the fly using Python.

Here is an example how to create a database and store some data in it:

```
import sqlite3

conn = sqlite3.connect("people.db")
cursor = conn.cursor()
cursor.execute("CREATE TABLE people (name TEXT, age INTEGER)")
cursor.execute("INSERT INTO people (name, age)
                VALUES ('Alice', 30)")
conn.commit()
conn.close()
```

The following code is used to read out the data from the database:

```
import sqlite3

conn = sqlite3.connect("people.db")
cursor = conn.cursor()
people = cursor.execute("SELECT * FROM people")
print(people.fetchall()) # prints [('Alice', 30)]
conn.commit()
conn.close()
```

SQL has been criticized for its syntax.[2] Passing commands as strings may have been a good idea in the 1970s, but nowadays, it is not. The problem is that you have to be very careful with the syntax. If you make a mistake, you get an error message that is not very helpful. Instead, it would be much better to have a proper API that checks the syntax and gives you a helpful error message. Though one could argue that in times of AI, this is not an issue anymore, but that's a different story.

Summary

We have now learned four of the most important file formats. So let me briefly summarize when you should use them.

CSV
CSV files can be used for flat data or if you want to open them in Excel, though I hope you'll learn enough Python here that you'll never have to use Excel again. Don't try to create structured data in CSV files; it will only lead to headaches.

JSON
JSON is great for storing structured data. It is a little bit more verbose than CSV, but it is much clearer what is stored in the file. JSON is a great choice for most of your data storage needs. JSON files can also be used as an interface between different libraries or even different programming languages.

---

[2] Robert C. Martin, https://x.com/unclebobmartin/status/1917558113177108537.

HDF5

HDF5 is very similar to JSON, but it is much more efficient. Therefore, HDF5 should be used if your data files are very large. HDF5 is used by large-scale research facilities and can easily store terabytes of data.

SQL

SQL is used to store large amounts of structured data that you have to query. In scientific computing, this is not the case too often unless you work on big data.

Time

In scientific computing, time may not be the most important thing. But when dealing with data from companies, it is paramount. And as many readers of this book will not end up in academia, but rather somewhere in the industry, I will also briefly cover the time module.

At first, working with time seems easy. You simply import the `time` module, and you are good to go.

```
import time

print(time.time()) # 1737400945.7503603
```

But here is the first surprise. You don't get a date back, but the time elapsed since January 1, 1970, measured in seconds. If you want a human-readable date, you have to use the `datetime` module.

```
import datetime

print(datetime.datetime.now()) # 2025-01-20 20:26:24.932706
```

Working with time or datetime also has some other pitfalls. The one I struggled with the most is the fact that the difference between two dates is not a date, but a `timedelta` object. This has its own set of complexities, and you have to be careful when working with it.

Also, time zones are something that you have to be aware of. This introduces all kinds of additional complexity. Giving you a general solution on how to deal with time zones is not possible. Many companies have tried to solve this problem with a very generic approach and have failed. You have to find a solution that is tailored to your needs.

Timing Functions

A common issue in scientific computing is "slow" code. In fact, code is never fast enough because scientists always want to simulate bigger systems.

In order to test the execution time of your code, you can use the `time` module. Here is an example of how to measure the execution time of a function:

```
import time

def slow_function():
    time.sleep(1)

start = time.time()
slow_function()
end = time.time()
print(end - start) # 1.0099
```

You can also define a so-called "decorator" to measure the execution time of a function. Decorators look like a cool thing, but they should be used sparingly. Too many decorators are like onion layers that you have to peel off to understand the code.

```
import time

def timing_decorator(func):
    def wrapper(*args, **kwargs):
        start = time.time()
        result = func(*args, **kwargs)
        end = time.time()
        print(f"Execution time: {end - start}")
        return result
    return wrapper

@timing_decorator
def slow_function():
    time.sleep(1)

slow_function() # Execution time: 1.0129
```

> **Performance**
> Code that is optimized for performance is generally hard to read. There are very few cases where performance is important. If you're using Python, you certainly don't have such a case. NumPy is comparably fast, but the rest of Python is quite slow. It is much more important to write good, maintainable, and readable code than code that is optimized for performance. Otherwise, the chances are high that you'll fail in the development phase of the software because of incomprehensible code.

Unit Tests   10

Tests are a piece of code that checks the actual code. It may, at first sight, seem a bit strange to write code that checks other code. But let me explain.

Why Tests?

The big question is: why should you even bother writing tests? After all, you used to get by without them.

That's true. But not everything was better in the past; on the contrary, software development has developed enormously in the last few decades. Writing tests is one of the reasons. Writing tests may sound like a lot of effort, which, admittedly, it is, but what is the alternative? In the past, people worked like this:

```
# in square.py
def square(x):
    return x**2

print(square(1)) # 1
print(square(2)) # 4
print(square(5)) # 25
```

This way of working works, of course, but it has a few very important disadvantages:

1. It is very error-prone because you have to manually check whether the results are correct.
2. These `print` statements are removed after the test, and in the future, nobody will know exactly what the code should do.

The second point, in particular, is extremely important. Code is changed several times during its lifetime, also known as refactoring (p. 9). The problem is that without tests, you can never be sure whether you have involuntarily changed the functionality of the code. In other words, whether you have introduced a bug. The only solution without tests is to omit refactoring. But in the long run, this leads to the code becoming a huge mess, as if you didn't clean your apartment for a year.

> **Unit Tests**
> Unit tests are time well invested. Of course, there is never a 100% guarantee that your code works. There's always something that can go wrong. But with proper unit test coverage, you get pretty close. Unit tests are probably the most effective way to ensure that your code works as expected.

How to Write Tests

As we have seen, the most common way for novice (and also many experienced) programmers is to use print statements and check by hand, and maybe with a calculator, that the results are correct.

```
# in square.py
def square(x):
    return x**2

print(square(1)) # 1
print(square(2)) # 4
print(square(5)) # 25
```

This process is dreadful. Apparently, this is something that can and should be automated. And this is exactly what unit tests are here for. The unit test for the corresponding code above would look like this:

```
# in square.py
def square(x):
    return x**2

# in test_square.py
from square import square
def test_square():
    assert square(1) == 1
    assert square(2) == 4
    assert square(5) == 25
```

That's it. All you had to do was replace the `print` statements with `assert` statements and place them into a test function and file. Pytest will look for everything that starts with `test_` and run it.

> **Do Not Repeat Yourself**
> The Do Not Repeat Yourself (DRY) principle states that you should never copy and paste code because you'll have redundancies in your code. This is bad because when you refactor it—and you certainly will have to at some point—you'll have to change the code in multiple places. This is error-prone.
> But the DRY principle also applies to procedural repetitions. *Everything* that you do more than once should be automated. This also includes the build, deployment, testing, etc. You should write tests for your code only once and then run them automatically.

You can run the test in the file `test_square.py` with the following command:

```
$ pytest test_square.py
```

Or, if you get an error message due to pytest, try

```
$ python -m pytest test_square.py
```

If you want to run all tests in the current directory, you can omit the file name, and pytest will run all tests in the current directory.

This should give you an output that looks roughly like this:

```
collected 1 item

test_square.py .

======== 1 passed in 2.61s ========
```

Now, of course, there's more to it—much more. As always, learning the basic syntax is the easiest part. The hard part is writing good tests.

The first question is: what are unit tests precisely?

> **Three Properties of Unit Tests**
>
> Unit tests have three properties. It is of utmost importance that you adhere to these properties. If you don't, your tests are useless.
>
> 1. They are fast, preferably within a few milliseconds.
> 2. They are deterministic and depend only on the code.
> 3. There are only two possible outcomes: pass or fail.

In your project, you will have hundreds, if not thousands, of unit tests that you will run all the time. This requires that your unit tests are fast. You don't want to wait more than a few seconds for them to finish. For this reason, a single unit test may take only a few milliseconds. This is an issue in Python, as Python is comparatively slow, and it may take more time to run all the tests. This is one of the reasons why I don't recommend using Python for large projects.

Flakiness is probably the worst property a test can have. If a test randomly fails once in a while, all your confidence in the test suite will be lost. For this reason, you have to make absolutely sure that your tests are deterministic. Your tests may never depend on any external factors like the file system or a network connection. You have to mock these things, as explained in the section on dependency injection on p. 97.

The third property implies that you always have to know the exact result of your calculation. A result cannot be "more or less correct." It's either correct or it's false. This is tested using `assert` statements. Tests without any `assert` statements are useless. They don't test anything, or even worse, they give you a wrong sense of security.

Tests that violate some of these properties can still be useful, but they no longer qualify as unit tests.

If possible, you should always write unit tests rather than something else. Unit tests are the gold standard of testing. Because why would you want to have slow, flaky tests if you can also have fast and stable tests? Only write other kinds of tests if you want to test something you cannot write a unit test for.

> **Check That Tests Fail**
> One of the worst cases is tests that don't fail even though they are supposed to. This may introduce all kinds of bugs into the system. For this reason, you should always check that tests fail if you expect them to.
>
> The best way to achieve this goal is by writing the tests upfront (see TDD, p. 94).

What to Test

When you write tests, the first question is always: which values should you test?

Obviously, it is not possible to test every value. Therefore, try to test all the corner cases and a few random values. For this reason, it is important that the author of the original code also writes the tests because they know the corner cases: dealing with empty lists, passing 0, etc. You can still make mistakes, but this way, you minimize the risk of missing something by a lot.

Now, this was the easy case: the one with only one variable. But if you have a function with multiple arguments, testing becomes a real nightmare. This is one of the reasons why functions should have few arguments. However, even if a function has only one argument, it can be a nested object containing many variables.

I hope you see the problem: testing code thoroughly is simply impossible. The test code in a well-tested system is at least as long as the actual code. In highly regulated industries, it can be several times as long. And it is still possible that you miss some corner cases.

The most important learning from this problem is that you should always keep the complexity of your code low. This is the only way to keep the number of bugs to a minimum. For example, you should always treat all elements of a list in the same way. In this way, you can test only one element, and you know that all other elements will most likely work as well.

> **Unit Tests and Good Code**
> Now this might come as a surprise to you, but unit tests not only help you find bugs. In fact, finding bugs is, in my opinion, the least important part of unit tests. A much more important part is that unit tests help you write good code. Normally, you write code and then start thinking about its interface. This is bad. It's the way Nokia designed its phones. They first built the phone and then tried to make it look good. This worked out until Apple reversed the development process and focused on the user experience first. You should do the same as Apple. First, design the interface and then implement the code accordingly. This results in code that is easy to use. And the tests force you to work this way.
>
> Good code is testable, and code that is not testable is bad.

Test-Driven Development

Test-Driven Development (TDD) is a way to write code. In TDD, you write your tests first and then implement the production code. Now, this might sound a little odd at the beginning, but it has its advantages. I also don't expect you to start with TDD right away; it takes some practice to write tests, so there is no need to rush it. But it's something you should keep in mind, especially if you know what you want to implement; it's a good idea to write the tests first.

The great thing about TDD is that it forces you even more to write good code than normal unit tests do. While it is still possible (though not so likely) that you write poorly tested code, with TDD, this is almost impossible. With TDD, you are *forced* to take the user's perspective of your code and design the interface accordingly. This *forces* you to write good code.

TDD consists of three steps that you repeat over and over again:

1. Write a failing test. If the test doesn't fail, investigate why.
2. Write just enough code to make the test pass. Don't write more code than necessary.
3. Refactor the code. Make sure it is clean and easy to understand.

Example of TDD

Let's make a short example. We want to write a function that returns the value of the Fizz Buzz game.[1] The Fizz Buzz game produces the following output: `1`, `2`, `"Fizz"`, `4`, `"Buzz"`, `"Fizz"`, `7`, `8`, `"Fizz"`, `"Buzz"`, `11`, `"Fizz"`, `13`, `14`, `"FizzBuzz"`, etc. I hope you get the idea.

We start by writing the first test to create the first element of the Fizz Buzz sequence.

```
# in test_fizzbuzz.py
from fizzbuzz import fizzbuzz

def test_fizzbuzz():
    assert fizzbuzz(1) == 1
```

This test fails because the function `fizzbuzz` doesn't exist yet. So we will implement the function.

```
# in fizzbuzz.py
def fizzbuzz(x):
    return 1
```

There is nothing to refactor, so we continue with the next test.

```
# in test_fizzbuzz.py
from fizzbuzz import fizzbuzz

def test_fizzbuzz():
    assert fizzbuzz(1) == 1
    assert fizzbuzz(2) == 2
```

The test fails, and therefore, we have to fix the code. We can simply fix the code by returning `x`.

```
# in fizzbuzz.py
def fizzbuzz(x):
    return x
```

Now comes the first difficulty: for the number 3, we should return "Fizz." So we write the test.

```
# in test_fizzbuzz.py
from fizzbuzz import fizzbuzz

def test_fizzbuzz():
    assert fizzbuzz(1) == 1
    assert fizzbuzz(2) == 2
    assert fizzbuzz(3) == "Fizz"
```

---

[1] https://en.wikipedia.org/wiki/Fizz_buzz

This requires an if statement in our code.

```python
# in fizzbuzz.py
def fizzbuzz(x):
    if x == 3:
        return "Fizz"
    return x
```

There is nothing to refactor.

As the test for 4 passes, we can write the test for 5 as well.

```python
# in test_fizzbuzz.py
from fizzbuzz import fizzbuzz

def test_fizzbuzz():
    assert fizzbuzz(1) == 1
    assert fizzbuzz(2) == 2
    assert fizzbuzz(3) == "Fizz"
    assert fizzbuzz(4) == 4
    assert fizzbuzz(5) == "Buzz"
```

The code is still quite simple and, so far, doesn't need any refactoring.

```python
# in fizzbuzz.py
def fizzbuzz(x):
    if x == 3:
        return "Fizz"
    if x == 5:
        return "Buzz"
    return x
```

The next step is to write the test for 6.

```python
# in test_fizzbuzz.py
from fizzbuzz import fizzbuzz

def test_fizzbuzz():
    assert fizzbuzz(1) == 1
    assert fizzbuzz(2) == 2
    assert fizzbuzz(3) == "Fizz"
    assert fizzbuzz(4) == 4
    assert fizzbuzz(5) == "Buzz"
    assert fizzbuzz(6) == "Fizz"
```

We first write very simple code to make the test pass.

```python
# in fizzbuzz.py
def fizzbuzz(x):
    if x == 3:
        return "Fizz"
    if x == 5:
        return "Buzz"
    if x == 6:
        return "Fizz"
    return x
```

Now we have some redundant code that we have to refactor. If $x\%3 == 0$, we have to return "Fizz." So we refactor the code accordingly.

```python
# in fizzbuzz.py
def fizzbuzz(x):
    if x % 3 == 0:
        return "Fizz"
    if x == 5:
        return "Buzz"
    return x
```

Here I stop with the example, as we have seen all three steps, and I don't want to fill the whole book with TDD. But I hope you have seen how TDD works and how it can help you write good code.

Dependency Injection

Dependency injection (DI) is an extremely useful tool to make your code testable. The idea is to pass all dependencies of a function as arguments instead of creating them inside the constructor. This way, you can replace the dependencies with mock objects in the test. Now, this might seem a bit abstract, and you might have to read this chapter a few times. First, we have to recapitulate what polymorphism and function objects are.

> **Polymorphism**
>
> As we have seen in the chapter on classes (p. 67), you can implement two classes with the same methods. These objects can then be used, for example, in a for loop. As long as all objects have the same methods, you can use them interchangeably. This is called polymorphism.
>
> ```python
> class A:
>     def some_function(self):
>         return 1
>
> class B:
>     def some_function(self):
>         return 2
>
> objects = [A(), B()]
> for obj in objects:
>     print(obj.some_function()) # prints 1 2
> ```
>
> In Python, polymorphism doesn't look like much. Meanwhile, in other languages like C++, it takes much more effort to achieve the same result.
>
> `A` and `B` both support the function `some_function`, and therefore, they can be used interchangeably in our code here. This may not seem very useful at first, but in fact, it is. Polymorphism can save you a lot of `if else` statements and is the basis of dependency injection (p. 97).

> **Function Objects**
>
> You can achieve similar behavior if you pass functions as arguments to other functions. This is called a function object.
>
> ```
> def function_one():
>     return 1
>
> def function_two():
>     return 2
>
> def print_function(func):
>     print(func())
>
> print_function(function_one) # prints 1
> print_function(function_two) # prints 2
> ```

Let's assume we have a file "numbers.txt" containing numbers separated by spaces, for example, "1 2 3 4 5". The following code reads the file and calculates the sum of these numbers:

```
def get_sum_of_file(file_name):
    with open(file_name) as f:
        content = f.read()
    numbers = content.split()
    return sum([int(number) for number in numbers])

print(get_sum_of_file("numbers.txt")) # prints 15
```

This is what every novice programmer writes. I wrote such code as well when I started programming, and it took me ages until I learned how to do it properly. Only when you look at the code through the eyes of an experienced programmer do you see a flaw: it is not possible to write unit tests for this code. This code relies on the existence of a file, and this is not allowed when writing unit tests. I hope I have your full attention because the following few pages are not so easy, but they are extremely important if you want to write serious software.

I hope I have already convinced you that unit tests are really important. So we need to change this code so that you can write unit tests for it. We have to get rid of the dependency on the file. There are several ways to do this, and there are still better and worse ways to do this.

Now the first thing to do is break the code into two functions. The first function reads the file, and the second function calculates the sum of the numbers. This way, we can test the second function without having to read the file.

```
def get_content(file_name):
    with open(file_name) as f:
        return f.read()

def get_sum_of_content(content):
    numbers = content.split()
    return sum([int(number) for number in numbers])

content = get_content("numbers.txt")
print(get_sum_of_content(content))
```

Now we can test `get_sum_of_content` without having to rely on the file system. This is certainly an improvement, as we can now write unit tests for this function. However, it won't be possible to test functions that call `get_sum_of_content` because we can't select the behavior of whether it should read a file or deal with some mocked data.

The code that most novices (including myself a long time ago) come up with looks like this:

```
def get_sum_of_content(content):
    numbers = content.split()
    return sum([int(number) for number in numbers])

def get_sum_of_file(file_name, use_real_data=True):
    if use_real_data:
        with open(file_name) as f:
            content = f.read()
    else:
        content = "1 2 3 4 5"
    return get_sum_of_content(content)

print(get_sum_of_file("numbers.txt")) # prints 15

# inside test_get_sum_of_file.py
assert get_sum_of_file("", False) == 15
```

But there is a better, more elegant way to achieve this goal: dependency injection (DI). The idea is to create an object that you can pass around instead of a Boolean. We have to create a polymorphic object where one implementation reads the file by executing the following code:

```
with open(file_name) as f:
    return f.read()
```

While the other function simply returns the mocked data.

```
return "1 2 3 4 5"
```

Then we have to write this code inside one function each. The final code can then choose to call either the first version of this code, reading a file in production, or call the second version of the code, returning the mock data. You can select which version of the code you want to execute by passing a function object to the function call. This is how the final code looks:

```
def get_sum_of_content(content):
    numbers = content.split()
    return sum([int(number) for number in numbers])

def get_content(file_name):
    with open(file_name) as f:
        return f.read()

def get_mock_content(file_name):
    return "1 2 3 4 5"

def get_sum_of_file(file_name, data_provider=get_content):
    content = data_provider(file_name)
    return get_sum_of_content(content)

print(get_sum_of_file("numbers.txt")) # prints 15

# inside test_get_sum_of_file.py
assert get_sum_of_file("", get_mock_content) == 15
```

When you see such code for the first time, you probably don't understand it. So let me explain what it does.

Let's start chronologically. The execution of the code starts with the function call of `get_sum_of_file`. This, in turn, calls the function we passed as an argument (`get_mock_content` for the test, the default function `get_content` for the real code).

For the real code, you can replace the line `content = data_provider(file_name)` with `content = get_content(file_name)` which will return the actual values of the file.

For the test code, this line will be replaced with

`content = get_mock_content("")` which will return the mock value "1 2 3 4 5".

The line `return get_sum_of_content(content)` will then calculate the sum of the numbers.

> **Advantages of Dependency Injection**
>
> Now, why is DI exactly so useful?
>
> The most obvious advantage of DI is that you don't need any `if` statements. This is always a good thing.
>
> Another advantage is that you can inject any behavior you want. Compared to the novice code above, you don't have to fiddle around with the implementation of the low-level code. You can simply replace the function that reads the file, and you're done.
>
> Your code becomes more modular as you can easily replace the injected code.
>
> Meanwhile, the only drawback that I see is the added complexity. Learning DI takes some time, but once you are used to it, this shouldn't be a problem. Just don't overdo it with DI. It's great for making things testable, but it's no panacea to fix all your code.

You can not only implement DI with functions, but you can also use classes. This is especially useful when you have to pass multiple dependencies to a function. In this case, you can create a class that stores all dependencies and pass this class to the function. The code looks very similar to the one above. The main difference is that for DI with classes, you have to define different classes that implement the same interface (i.e., they have the same methods).

```python
def get_sum_of_content(content):
    numbers = content.split()
    return sum([int(number) for number in numbers])

class RealContentProvider(file_name):
    def get_content(file_name):
        with open(file_name) as f:
            return f.read()

class MockContentProvider:
    def get_content(file_name):
        return "1 2 3 4 5"

def get_sum_of_file(file_name,
                    data_provider=RealContentProvider()):
    content = data_provider.get_content(file_name)
    return get_sum_of_content(content)

print(get_sum_of_file("numbers.txt")) # prints 15

# inside test_get_sum_of_file.py
assert get_sum_of_file("", MockContentProvider()) == 15
```

If you understood the function approach, you should have no problem understanding the class approach. But let's go through the code once again.

The code execution starts with the function call of `get_sum_of_file`.
In the test, the argument of this function is an object of type
`MockContentProvider`; for the real code, the argument is the default value of `RealContentProvider`.

In the line `content = data_provider.get_content(file_name)`, you'll have to replace the `data_provider` object with the actual object. This is either `RealContentProvider` or `MockContentProvider`. So you have either the function call `RealContentProvider().get_content(file_name)` for the actual code or `MockContentProvider().get_content(file_name)` for the test code. This code returns the value of the corresponding method.

As I've already written, the advantage of class-based DI is that you can define many methods within the classes. This allows you to create much more sophisticated behavior when mocking the data. But in most cases, the functional approach is sufficient.

Mocking

Once you implement DI, mocking is really simple. The idea behind it is that you take a complicated function that might need access to the file system or have other bad side effects and replace it with a very simple piece of code. This simple piece of code is called a mock. The mock should return a predefined value and not have any side effects. Mocking combined with DI is the best combination when you want to test functions that have side effects that are difficult to deal with.

Faking

Faking is a much more elaborate technique than mocking. With faking, you replace a function with a completely different implementation. For example, you replace a database with an in-memory database that you wrote to mimic the behavior of the real database. Faking is a very powerful technique, but it is also very complex. It is only used in very rare cases.

Here is a very simple example of such a fake database. It supports only an `insert` and a `get` method, but that might be sufficient for many tests.

```python
class FakeDatabase:
    def __init__(self):
        self.data = {}

    def insert(self, key, value):
        self.data[key] = value

    def get(self, key):
        return self.data[key]
```

Matplotlib 11

While the code so far has covered the very basics of programming with Python, we will now have a look at a completely different topic: the Matplotlib library.

If you work with a lot of data, it is generally useful to display it graphically. Just having a bunch of data points alone is fairly useless because you won't see the relevant information from the numbers alone. If you have a bunch of numbers, it is generally advisable to plot them until you see some interesting patterns. And this is exactly what Matplotlib is for. Matplotlib is the plotting library for Python. It offers a lot of functionality and can do pretty much everything you want. I will therefore not be able to cover all its functionality in this book, but will only explain the basic examples. If you need to create a plot that requires more functionality, I recommend you take a look at the Matplotlib gallery.[1] Search for examples that look similar to what you want to achieve and then adapt the code to your needs by experimenting with it. The code you write this way may not be elegant, but plotting code usually doesn't have to be.

Simple Plots

Here is a simple example that shows how to plot a simple curve. Note that Matplotlib accepts both normal lists as well as numpy arrays. Use whatever type you have at hand.

A plot is, roughly speaking, a sequence of points connected by lines. For each point, you need an x- and y-coordinate. The x-coordinate is the horizontal position of the point, and the y-coordinate is the vertical position of the point. Here is an example of a sine curve as seen in Figure 11.1:

```
import matplotlib.pyplot as plt
import numpy as np

plt.rcParams.update({'font.size': 12})

x = np.linspace(0, 10, 100)
y = np.sin(x)
plt.plot(x, y)
plt.show()
```

---

[1] https://matplotlib.org/stable/gallery/index.html

Fig. 11.1 A simple plot of the sine function

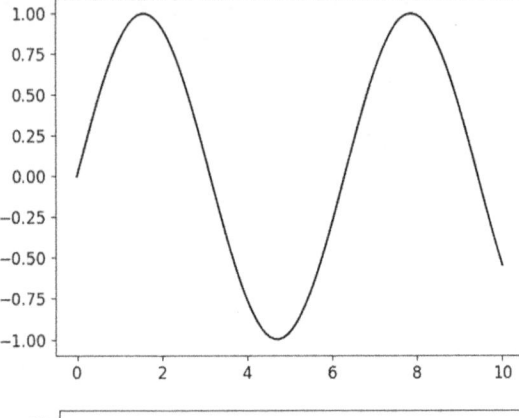

Fig. 11.2 Two curves in one plot

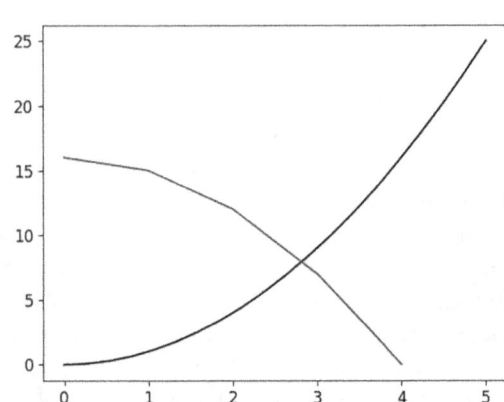

That the line `plt.rcParams.update('font.size': 12)` adjusts the font size of the plot. This is not required, but I do so because the default font size is too small for this book. I will omit this line in the following examples as it doesn't add anything to the code. I'm just mentioning this so that you are not confused about why your plots don't look 100% exactly the same as the ones in this book.

The basic functionality of Matplotlib is as follows: You plot different data with the `plt.plot()` function. You can also call this function several times if you want to display different data in the same plot. Whenever you call `plt.show()`, all the data that you have selected with `plt.plot()` is displayed graphically. This way, you can display different data in one plot at the same time, or you can also create several different plots with one program. Here is an example that graphically displays several datasets at once:

```
import matplotlib.pyplot as plt
import numpy as np

x1 = np.linspace(0,5,20)
y1 = x1**2
x2 = np.linspace(0,4,5)
y2 = 16-x2**2
plt.plot(x1, y1)
plt.plot(x2, y2)
plt.show()
```

The result of this code can be seen in Figure 11.2.

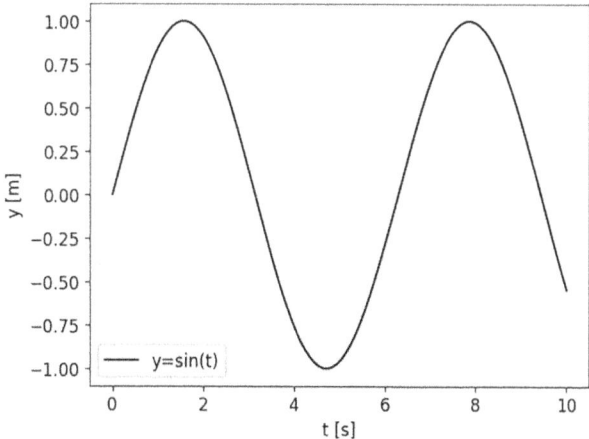

Fig. 11.3 A plot with a label

Labeling

A plot is not worth much if the axes are not labeled because, without axis labels, we are missing important information. And while we're at it, we can also label the curve.

```
import matplotlib.pyplot as plt
import numpy as np

t = np.linspace(0,10,100)
y = sin(t)
plt.plot(t,y, label='y=sin(t)')
plt.xlabel("t [s]")
plt.ylabel("y [m]")
plt.legend()
plt.show()
```

The result of this code can be seen in Figure 11.3. Usually, the label of the curve would be located at the top right, but it would intersect with the curve. So, Matplotlib moved it to the bottom left.

> **Labels**
> Always label the axes of your plots. Plots without labels are worthless. And don't forget the units!

Histograms

A histogram is used when you want to graphically display the frequency of an event at different values. For example, let's create a Gaussian distribution using 1,000 random numbers. The result can be seen in Figure 11.4

```
import random
import matplotlib.pyplot as plt

random.seed(1)
```

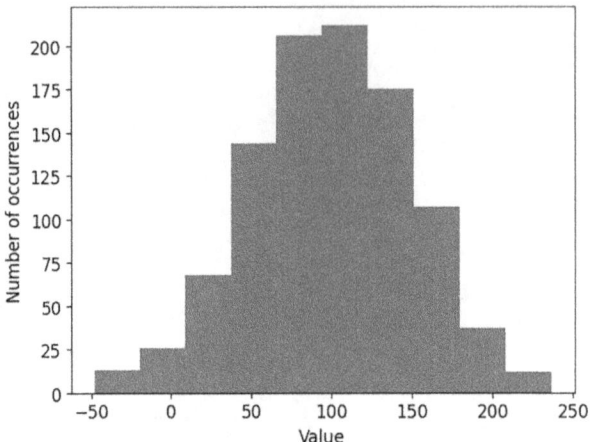

Fig. 11.4 A histogram of a Gaussian distribution

```
mu = 100
sigma = 50
nums = [random.gauss(mu, sigma) for _ in range(1000)]

plt.hist(nums, bins=10)
plt.xlabel('Value')
plt.ylabel('Number of occurrences')
plt.show()
```

If you want to have the exact data that this histogram corresponds to, you can get it with the code

```
n, bins, _ = plt.hist(data, bins=10)
```

This way, you can also create a curve instead of a histogram, but you don't have to forego the convenience of the histogram functionality. The plots, histograms, etc., of Matplotlib often return objects that correspond to the plot or the data generated for the histogram. In this case, we can use the variables n, bins, _ to access the data generated for the histogram. n corresponds to the y-values, and bins corresponds to the x-values.

```
n, bins, _ = plt.hist(data, bins=30)
bin_average = (bins[1:] + bins[:-1]) / 2
plt.clf()
plt.plot(bin_average, n)
```

The plt.clf() line here was used to remove the histogram from the plot since I only want the curve to be displayed. Accordingly, I had to discard the histogram.

Curve Fitting

It happens often that you want to find a parameter of a function based on a set of data points. This generally requires you to do a curve fit.

In this example, we throw an object into the air and measure its position as a function of time. From the fitted curve, we will determine the initial position, the initial velocity, and the gravitational acceleration. We fake the data by calculating the accurate values and adding Gaussian noise to it. Then we use the curve_fit function from the scipy.optimize package to fit the data and plot it.

Curve Fitting

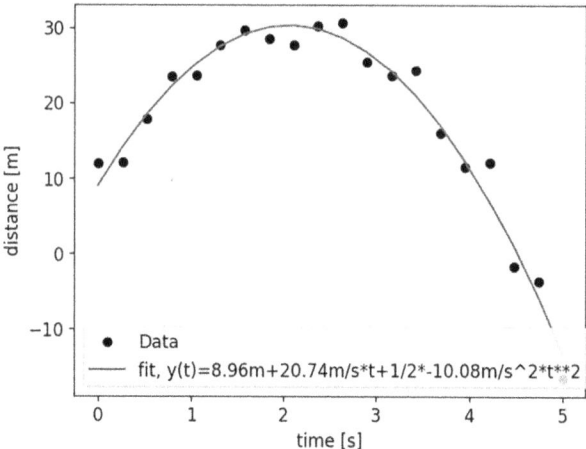

Fig. 11.5 The blue dots are the simulated data, the orange curve is the fitted curve

Curve fitting is invaluable for scientists and engineers. I highly recommend you play around with this code and try to fit different functions to your data.

```
import matplotlib.pyplot as plt
import numpy as np
import random
from scipy.optimize import curve_fit

random.seed(0)
t = np.linspace(0, 5, 20)
s_0 = 10
v_0 = 20
a = -9.81

def f(t, s_0, v_0, a):
    return s_0 + v_0*t + 1/2*a*t**2
y = [f(i, s_0, v_0, a) + random.gauss(0, 2) for i in t]

popt, pcov = curve_fit(f, t, y, p0=[10, 20, -10])

plt.plot(t, y, 'o')
plt.plot(t, f(t, *popt))
plt.xlabel('time [s]')
plt.ylabel('distance [m]')
plt.legend(['Data', f'fit,
    y(t)={popt[0]:.2f}m+{popt[1]:.2f}m/s*t+
        1/2*{popt[2]:.2f}m/s^2*t**2'])
plt.plot()
```

The result of this code can be seen in Figure 11.5. The round dots are the simulated data points, meanwhile the solid line is the fitted curve.

It is important to not only publish the fitted values that we have access to with the structured variable `popt`, but also how stable the fit is. This information can be obtained in two ways. The mathematical one is the covariance matrix `pcov` that we obtained from the curve fitting. "High" values of the covariance matrix indicate that the fit is not very stable and should be looked at more closely.

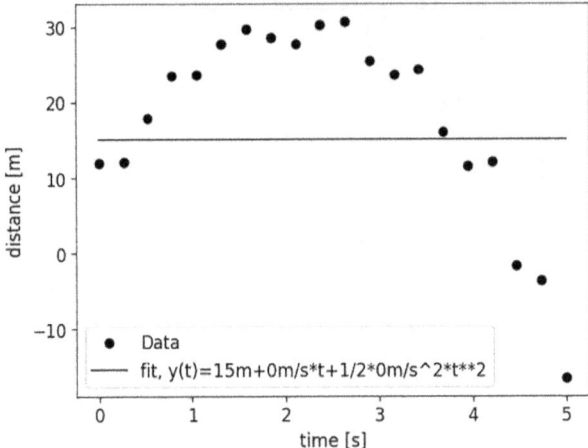

Fig. 11.6 This is an example of a bad fit

The other method to judge the quality of a fit is very profound. Create a plot with the data and look at it. You'll see immediately the quality of the fit. One plot says more than a thousand numbers.

> **Curve Fitting and Machine Learning**
> Some people do curve fitting and claim to be doing machine learning. In my opinion, this is false because there is no learning effect involved. On the other hand, machine learning is also about finding patterns in data. So, curve fitting and machine learning share some similarities.

Local Minima of Curve Fitting

It is always recommended that you check the fit parameters when doing curve fitting because even if your data looks fine, the algorithm may get stuck in a local minimum and return a bad fit.

In Figure 11.6, you can see an example of how a bad fit could look. The fit obviously doesn't align with the data.

I didn't manage to create a bad fit deliberately, so I just added a random curve for demonstration purposes. But this doesn't mean that bad fits are an exception. If the starting values of the fit are poorly chosen, this happens at times and without any apparent reason. So always check the fit parameters and the covariance matrix, or create a plot where you can see the data and the fit.

Pandas

12

Pandas is a library for data analysis and manipulation. It provides data structures and functions for working with structured data, such as tables and time series. Pandas is built on top of NumPy and provides a more user-friendly interface for working with data.

The fact that Pandas is based on NumPy allows the user to deal with large datasets in an efficient way as the NumPy library is highly optimized for performance.

Now, of course, you could also do everything using NumPy instead of Pandas. It would just be a lot more work and less user-friendly.

Pandas Example

I think it is best understood what Pandas can do by looking at an example. Here is a dataset that I found somewhere on the internet. It's far from perfect, but it's a good example for what Pandas can do.

At the beginning, the dataset is barely readable as it is not formatted in a human-readable way. It is anyway not recommended that you read pure data files to begin with. After a little bit of processing the data, you'll get a much better overview.

Also note that there is no clear goal on what we want to achieve with this dataset. The only goal I have is to show you what Pandas can do.

```
Date   Company Person Name Room number
1-Jan-2022 Avamba Anatole Ridehalgh 4008
1-Jan-2022 Fatz Aldrich McKevin 2002
1-Jan-2022 Leexo Stanley Hadrill 4012
Hotels
1-Jan-2022 Rhyzio Lyndell Tice 1006
1-Jan-2022 Eadel Broderic Handscombe 3015
1-Jan-2022 Oozz Deina Harwin 2005
1-Jan-2022 Innotype Benyamin Crocetti 2001
1-Jan-2022 Thea Melan 5006
1-Jan-2022 Alexei Kneale 3002
1-Jan-2022 Jayo Tate Manntschke 3014
Booking
...
```

Our dataset has a few issues. For example, there are entries without a company name. Furthermore, it isn't clear at first sight what the "Hotels" and "Booking" rows are. Obviously these lines are special. My guess is that "Hotels" and "Booking" are just the names of the companies that are booking the rooms. The booking companies seem to be always written below the associated rows. This is bad as it's hard to understand the data at first sight. The data should be written in a proper csv format or a json file.

The missing entries don't worry me too much as the values will be filled with a NaN value. What bothers me most are the booking companies and how we have to process them.

Let's first read in the data.

```
import pandas as pd
import numpy as np

data = pd.read_csv('data.txt', sep='\t')
print(data.head(12))
```

The result looks as follows. Now it's also properly formatted and you can better understand the structure of the data.

```
         Date   Company         Person Name  Room number
0   1-Jan-2022    Avamba    Anatole Ridehalgh       4008.0
1   1-Jan-2022      Fatz     Aldrich McKevin        2002.0
2   1-Jan-2022     Leexo     Stanley Hadrill        4012.0
3       Hotels       NaN                   NaN         NaN
4   1-Jan-2022    Rhyzio        Lyndell Tice       1006.0
5   1-Jan-2022     Eadel  Broderic Handscombe       3015.0
6   1-Jan-2022      Oozz        Deina Harwin       2005.0
7   1-Jan-2022  Innotype    Benyamin Crocetti       2001.0
8   1-Jan-2022       NaN          Thea Melan       5006.0
9   1-Jan-2022       NaN       Alexei Kneale       3002.0
10  1-Jan-2022      Jayo     Tate Manntschke       3014.0
11     Booking       NaN                   NaN         NaN
```

As second step, we want to add the booking company to every line. First we have to filter out the lines that are not booking lines.

```
mask = data['Room number'].isna()
print(mask.head(12))
```

This will return a Boolean mask that is true for all rows where the "Room number" column is NaN.

```
0     False
1     False
2     False
3      True
4     False
5     False
6     False
7     False
8     False
9     False
10    False
11     True
```

The following line of code creates a new column called "text_value" that contains the value of the "Date" column for all rows where the "Room number" column is NaN. Otherwise, it contains NaN.

```
data['text_value'] = np.where(mask, data['Date'], np.nan)
print(data['text_value'].head(12))
```

```
0        NaN
1        NaN
2        NaN
3      Hotels
4        NaN
5        NaN
6        NaN
7        NaN
8        NaN
9        NaN
10       NaN
11     Booking
```

The next step requires some knowledge of Pandas. We want to fill the NaN values with the next non-NaN value. This can be done with the function `bfill`. This name is an abbreviation for "backward fill."

```
data['text_value'] = data['text_value'].bfill()
print(data['text_value'].head(12))
```

Note that we had to assign the result back to the column as `bfill` does not modify the column in place. It only returns the modified column.

```
0      Hotels
1      Hotels
2      Hotels
3      Hotels
4      Booking
5      Booking
6      Booking
7      Booking
8      Booking
9      Booking
10     Booking
11     Booking
```

We can also look at the complete data.

```
print(data.head(12))
```

	Date	Company	Person Name	Room number	text_value
0	1-Jan-2022	Avamba	Anatole Ridehalgh	4008.0	Hotels
1	1-Jan-2022	Fatz	Aldrich McKevin	2002.0	Hotels
2	1-Jan-2022	Leexo	Stanley Hadrill	4012.0	Hotels
3	Hotels	NaN	NaN	NaN	Hotels
4	1-Jan-2022	Rhyzio	Lyndell Tice	1006.0	Booking
5	1-Jan-2022	Eadel	Broderic Handscombe	3015.0	Booking
6	1-Jan-2022	Oozz	Deina Harwin	2005.0	Booking
7	1-Jan-2022	Innotype	Benyamin Crocetti	2001.0	Booking
8	1-Jan-2022	NaN	Thea Melan	5006.0	Booking
9	1-Jan-2022	NaN	Alexei Kneale	3002.0	Booking
10	1-Jan-2022	Jayo	Tate Manntschke	3014.0	Booking
11	Booking	NaN	NaN	NaN	Booking

Note that I tweaked the format a little to make it fit into the page width. The code we used above with `data['text_value']` already added a new column to the data frame, so we didn't need an additional assignment.

Now comes the question how to deal with the NaN values in our data. There is no unique solution to this problem. Therefore, it is important that we are aware of what we want to achieve.

Now, we certainly want to remove the lines like this one: `3 Hotels NaN NaN NaN Hotels`. So we could remove all lines that contain a `NaN` using the `dropna()` function. This, however, would remove all lines that contain a `NaN` in any column, including lines like `8 1-Jan-2022 NaN Thea Melan 5006.0 Booking`. Whether we want to do so depends on the specific problem we are trying to solve. If we want to process only entries with a valid company name, we can do so. Though I would recommend against it. By removing the lines with `NaN` values, we would do two things in one step: we would remove the booking page lines and filter out the invalid companies. It is generally recommended to do only one thing at a time. So let's start by removing the booking page lines. This can be done using the element wise not operator ~ on the mask and use it as a Boolean index.

```
data = data[~mask]
data.head(12)
```

Admittedly, I had to use my AI tool to generate this code. I didn't come up with this trick by myself.

```
         Date    Company       Person Name  Room number  text_value
0   1-Jan-2022     Avamba  Anatole Ridehalgh       4008.0      Hotels
1   1-Jan-2022       Fatz    Aldrich McKevin       2002.0      Hotels
2   1-Jan-2022      Leexo    Stanley Hadrill       4012.0      Hotels
4   1-Jan-2022     Rhyzio      Lyndell Tice       1006.0     Booking
5   1-Jan-2022      Eadel  Broderic Handscombe    3015.0     Booking
6   1-Jan-2022       Oozz      Deina Harwin       2005.0     Booking
7   1-Jan-2022   Innotype  Benyamin Crocetti      2001.0     Booking
8   1-Jan-2022        NaN         Thea Melan      5006.0     Booking
9   1-Jan-2022        NaN      Alexei Kneale      3002.0     Booking
10  1-Jan-2022       Jayo    Tate Manntschke      3014.0     Booking
12  1-Jan-2022        NaN      Eudora Nettle      6003.0    Cleartrip
13  1-Jan-2022   Riffpedia     Elianore Vigar     3002.0    Cleartrip
```

One thing that bothered me for quite a while is the fact that the `Room number` column is of type `float` and not `int`. This is because the `NaN` values are of type `float`. To fix this, we can use the `astype` function. As we have already removed all the `NaN` entries, this is now quite simple.

```
data['Room number'] = data['Room number'].astype(int)
print(data.head(12))
```

```
         Date      Company       Person Name  Room number  text_value
0   1-Jan-2022       Avamba  Anatole Ridehalgh         4008      Hotels
1   1-Jan-2022         Fatz    Aldrich McKevin         2002      Hotels
2   1-Jan-2022        Leexo    Stanley Hadrill         4012      Hotels
4   1-Jan-2022       Rhyzio      Lyndell Tice           1006     Booking
5   1-Jan-2022        Eadel  Broderic Handscombe        3015     Booking
6   1-Jan-2022         Oozz      Deina Harwin           2005     Booking
7   1-Jan-2022     Innotype  Benyamin Crocetti          2001     Booking
10  1-Jan-2022         Jayo    Tate Manntschke          3014     Booking
13  1-Jan-2022    Riffpedia     Elianore Vigar          3002    Cleartrip
14  1-Jan-2022         Tazz     Alonso Mundee           4006    Cleartrip
16  1-Jan-2022   Browsezoom     Ysabel Lordon           6003      Hotels
17  1-Jan-2022       Skinte     Raff Verecker           3012      Hotels
```

In the following, we no longer need the "Company" column. It only uses some of the precious space in this book. We can drop it.

```
data.drop(columns=['Company'], inplace=True)
print(data.head(12))
```

```
        Date        Person Name  Room number  text_value
0   1-Jan-2022    Anatole Ridehalgh         4008       Hotels
1   1-Jan-2022    Aldrich McKevin           2002       Hotels
2   1-Jan-2022    Stanley Hadrill           4012       Hotels
4   1-Jan-2022    Lyndell Tice              1006      Booking
5   1-Jan-2022    Broderic Handscombe       3015      Booking
6   1-Jan-2022    Deina Harwin              2005      Booking
7   1-Jan-2022    Benyamin Crocetti         2001      Booking
10  1-Jan-2022    Tate Manntschke           3014      Booking
13  1-Jan-2022    Elianore Vigar            3002     Cleartrip
14  1-Jan-2022    Alonso Mundee             4006     Cleartrip
16  1-Jan-2022    Ysabel Lordon             6003       Hotels
17  1-Jan-2022    Raff Verecker             3012       Hotels
```

All the dates in the table are identical. For the sake of making this example a little bit more interesting, we will create dates that are three days apart. This gives us something to play with. Now, of course, you shouldn't do such a random operation with your actual data. This is only for illustration purposes.

```
data['Date'] = pd.date_range(start='1/1/2022', periods=len(data), freq='3D')
print(data.head(12))
```

```
         Date         Person Name  Room number  text_value
0   2022-01-01    Anatole Ridehalgh         4008       Hotels
1   2022-01-04    Aldrich McKevin           2002       Hotels
2   2022-01-07    Stanley Hadrill           4012       Hotels
4   2022-01-10    Lyndell Tice              1006      Booking
5   2022-01-13    Broderic Handscombe       3015      Booking
6   2022-01-16    Deina Harwin              2005      Booking
7   2022-01-19    Benyamin Crocetti         2001      Booking
10  2022-01-22    Tate Manntschke           3014      Booking
13  2022-01-25    Elianore Vigar            3002     Cleartrip
14  2022-01-28    Alonso Mundee             4006     Cleartrip
16  2022-01-31    Ysabel Lordon             6003       Hotels
17  2022-02-03    Raff Verecker             3012       Hotels
```

We can also create some new data based on the current data. For example, we can create a new column called "price" that contains the price of the room. Again, it doesn't make much sense, but for the sake of making this example interesting, our price is depending on the room number, as well as the month of the year.

```
data['price'] = 100 + data['Room number']//100 +
                data['Date'].dt.month
```

```
         Date         Person Name  Room number  text_value  price
0   2022-01-01    Anatole Ridehalgh         4008       Hotels    141
1   2022-01-04    Aldrich McKevin           2002       Hotels    121
2   2022-01-07    Stanley Hadrill           4012       Hotels    141
4   2022-01-10    Lyndell Tice              1006      Booking    111
5   2022-01-13  Broderic Handscombe         3015      Booking    131
6   2022-01-16    Deina Harwin              2005      Booking    121
7   2022-01-19    Benyamin Crocetti         2001      Booking    121
10  2022-01-22    Tate Manntschke           3014      Booking    131
13  2022-01-25    Elianore Vigar            3002     Cleartrip    131
14  2022-01-28    Alonso Mundee             4006     Cleartrip    141
16  2022-01-31    Ysabel Lordon             6003       Hotels    161
17  2022-02-03    Raff Verecker             3012       Hotels    132
```

Besides editing values in the table, as done so far, we can also calculate key indicators. For example, we can count the number of rooms, calculate the total price of all rooms, or calculate the correlation between the price and the month.

```
number_of_bookings = data['price'].count()
print(f"number_of_bookings = {number_of_bookings}")
# number_of_bookings = 134
total_price = data['price'].sum()
print(f"total_price = {total_price}")
# total_price = 18148
corr = data['price'].corr(data['Date'].dt.month)
print(f"Correlation between price and month = {corr}")
# Correlation between price and dayofweek = 0.10408429277227432
```

As expected, there is some positive correlation between the price and the month. This is because the price relates positively to the month.

Sorting the data by price is done as follows:

```
data = data.sort_values(by='price', ascending=False)
print(data.head(12))
```

	Date	Person Name	Room number	text_value	price
166	2022-12-12	Licha Attyeo	7002	Hotels	182
118	2022-09-01	Dukey Hansod	7001	Expedia	179
33	2022-03-08	Alric Reeder	7001	Agent 007	173
151	2022-11-15	Marty Jerome	6001	Booking	171
187	2023-01-26	Victoria Lavery	7002	Expedia	171
184	2023-01-17	George Downgate	7001	Expedia	171
88	2022-07-09	M. Crathern	6001	Booking	167
59	2022-05-04	Dorita Boulger	6005	Hotels	165
55	2022-04-25	K. Shaughnessy	6003	Agent 007	164
54	2022-04-22	Sherlock Hyland	6001	Agent 007	164
22	2022-02-12	Howey Oseman	6001	Expedia	162
171	2022-12-24	Vivianna Syvret	5005	Cleartrip	162

This example was somewhat artificial. I just took a random dataset and applied whatever operation on it that I wanted to show you. In reality, you'll have to take the opposite approach: you'll have to understand the problem first and then apply the appropriate operations to solve it.

Numerical Mathematics 13

This chapter deals with one of the most important topics in software development: numerical mathematics. You will see that the difficulty of software development lies mainly in understanding a problem, not in implementing the solution. The code examples here are mostly quite short compared to the explanations of the problem.

One of the most important tasks in software development is numerical calculations on a large scale. This is because, for many mathematical formulas, there is no exact solution. One of the most important examples is the Navier-Stokes equation, which describes the behavior of fluids. It forms the basis of aerodynamics and, thus, of the entire aircraft industry.

> **The Navier-Stokes Equation**
> Here is the short notation of the Navier-Stokes momentum equation for compressible flow:[a]
>
> $$\rho \frac{D\mathbf{u}}{Dt} = \rho \left(\frac{\partial \mathbf{u}}{\partial t} + (\mathbf{u} \cdot \nabla)\mathbf{u} \right) \tag{13.1}$$
>
> The Navier-Stokes equation is one of the seven millennial problems of the Clay Mathematics Institute. For making considerable progress in solving this equation, a prize of one million dollars is awarded. And the aerospace industry would certainly be willing to pay you a lot more than that.
>
> ---
> [a]https://en.wikipedia.org/wiki/Navier%E2%80%93Stokes_equations

The Navier-Stokes equation is a second-order inhomogeneous differential equation for which no exact solution is generally known in the general case, and it can only be calculated approximately. This means that it is possible to determine certain problems very precisely, such as calculating the drag and lift values of wing profiles, but at the same time, the prediction of the angle at which the flow around the wing will break off is still quite inaccurate. The calculation of three-dimensional objects is extremely computationally intensive and, until a few years ago, was only possible for the simplest cases or in two dimensions. Despite all the advances in algorithms and the constantly increasing performance of supercomputers, it is still unavoidable that prototypes are produced in aerodynamics and measured in reality or in wind tunnels.

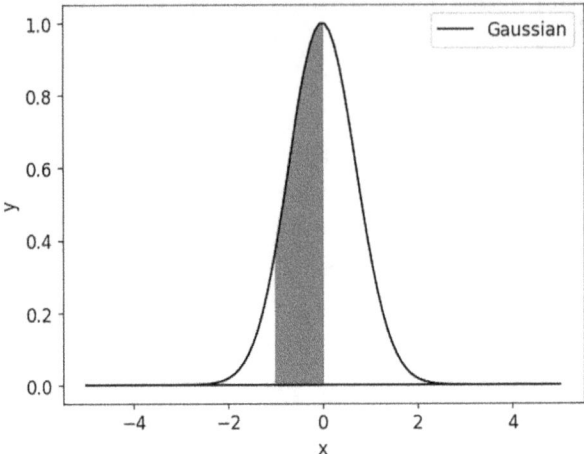

Fig. 13.1 The black curve is the Gaussian function. The gray area is its integral from -1 to 0

In the following, we will solve a few mathematical problems numerically using Python. It is not so important whether you understand all the mathematics behind it. The examples have been chosen so that you should be able to understand them roughly even without in-depth knowledge of mathematics.

Numerical Integration

The term "integration" refers to the mathematical method of determining "the area under a curve", as can be seen for example in Figure 13.1. This is only possible analytically, i.e., with pure mathematics, in certain cases. Often, you have to approximate this numerically with a certain degree of accuracy. You can look at the problem from two different points of view. You can either approximate the integral by calculating the area under the curve, or you can calculate the Riemann sum. Both methods are equivalent and will be explained in the following.

A well-known example is the Gaussian bell curve, which cannot be integrated analytically. Only a few special cases are known exactly. For example, the total area under the Gaussian bell curve is exactly 1. The constant factor of the Gaussian bell curve can be calculated exactly and was chosen accordingly.

Mathematical Derivation

The integral can be approximated by the Riemann sum:

$$\int_a^b f(x)dx = \lim_{n \to \inf} \sum_{i=0}^{n-1} \frac{(b-a)}{n} f(x_i), \tag{13.2}$$

The only tricky part is to determine the support points x_i. I will not give you the mathematical formula for the support points, as it becomes quite complicated. Instead, I will give you a rough explanation of how to calculate them. The resulting code is much easier than the mathematical formula.

Numerical Integration

1. First, we have to split the interval $[a, b]$ into n parts. This is done by the code `x = np.linspace(a, b, n)`.
2. Then we have to calculate the midpoints of the intervals. For this purpose, we calculate the average of the neighboring points. This is done by the code `x_average = (x[1:] + x[:-1])/2`. Note that the length of the list `x_average` is $n - 1$.

Geometric Interpretation

As already mentioned, it is also possible to derive the formula 13.2 geometrically by approximating the area under the curve with rectangles. The width of the rectangles is given by $\frac{b-a}{n}$ and the height by the function value at the support points. The area of the rectangles is then the sum of the areas of the rectangles, as shown in Figure 13.2.

The edges of the rectangles are located at $a + i \cdot \frac{b-a}{n}$ where $i = 0, 1, 2, \ldots, n$. The support points are the same as calculated in the mathematical derivation. Therefore, the final formula for the integral is also the same as in the mathematical derivation.

$$\int_a^b f(x)dx \approx \sum_{i=0}^{n-1} h_i \cdot w = \sum_{i=0}^{n-1} f(x_i) \cdot \frac{b-a}{n} \tag{13.3}$$

Now this looks all quite complicated, but I find it much clearer when looking at the code. Especially, calculating the support points is quite simple if you know some list slicing tricks.

```
x = np.linspace(-1, 0, 4)
x_support = (x[1:]+ x[:-1])/2
```

These two lines of code pretty much solve the problem and save us a lot of mathematical calculations. We calculate the edges of the squares in the first line and the midpoints in the second line using list slicing. The rest of the code is straightforward, using Python's built-in `sum` function.

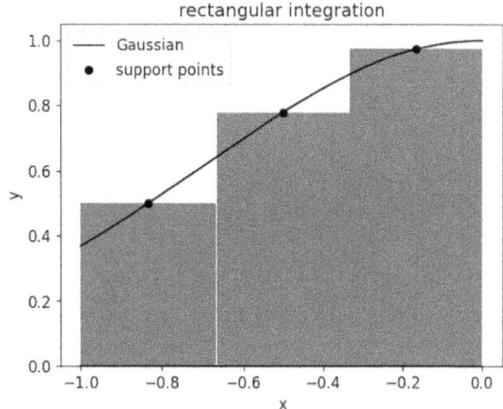

Fig. 13.2 The integral of the Gaussian function from $-.1$ to 0 calculated with the rectangle rule. The shape of the Gaussian function is shown with the dark line, the support points are shown with black circles, the calculated are with this formula is shown in gray

```
def gauss(x):
    return np.exp(-x**2)

width = 1./3
height = gauss(x_support)
I = sum(height*width) # results in 0.750
```

> **Understanding the Problem**
>
> If you are disappointed that I have now explained so much about numerical integration to you, but the actual code is only about seven lines long, I have to tell you that this is quite normal in software development. It is often more difficult to find out exactly what you have to do than to write the actual code. And if writing the code is difficult, you should probably rethink your approach.
>
> The gray box on requirements engineering on p. 72 goes in the same direction: finding out what you have to do is often more difficult than implementing it.
>
> You should *never* write code if you haven't understood the problem that you are trying to solve. Writing code won't help you in any way. You will only get confused and get wrong results.

Higher Order Integration

Another way of calculating the integral numerically is by approximating the area with slanted squares. This takes a little bit more effort to implement than the previous method, but it is generally more accurate. This is also called the trapezoidal rule. The general idea is shown in Figure 13.3.

If you sum up the areas of all the trapezoids, you'll see that the weight of the first and the last support points is one, while all points in between have a weight of two.

```
x = np.linspace(-1, 0, 4)
width = 1
n_weights = 6
I = width * (gauss(x[0]) + gauss(x[-1]) + 2*np.sum(gauss(x[1:-1])))/n_weights
          # results in 0.740
```

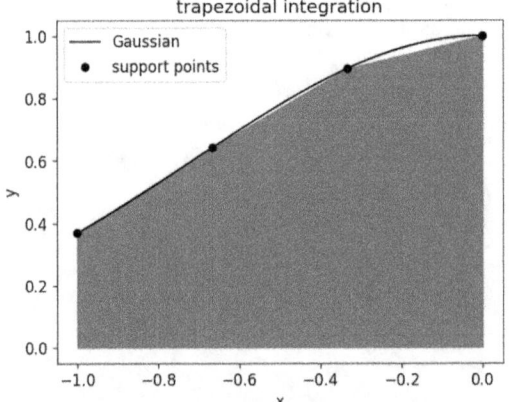

Fig. 13.3 The integral of the Gaussian function from − .1 to 0 calculated with the trapezoidal rule. The shape of the Gaussian function is shown with the dark line, the support points are shown with black circles, the calculated are with this formula is shown in gray

Numerical Integration

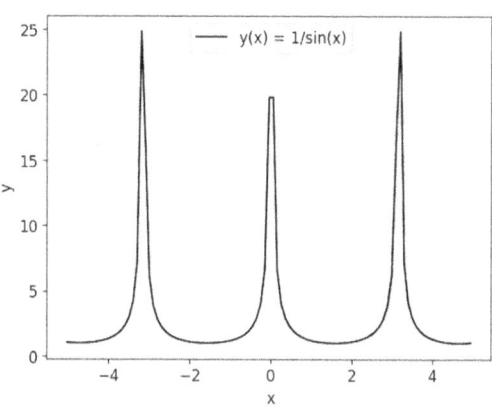

Fig. 13.4 An example of a function that is difficult to integrate numerically as it diverges at some points

There are also methods of an even higher order, which are even more precise. The interested reader can find these in any book on numerical mathematics.

Estimating the Accuracy

As always in numerical mathematics, the question arises as to how precise a result is. Of course, you can make it more precise by using more support points, but the question is now how precise it has to be and when this accuracy is achieved.

The most obvious thing that influences the accuracy is the number of support points. For $lim_{n \to \infty}$, the Riemann sum converges to the integral, so we should get an accurate result.

A property that influences the accuracy of the numerical integration is how uniform the function is. In Figure 13.4, we have the function $1/abs(sin(x))$, which diverges at the points 0, pi, etc. (it is not defined for these points or tends toward infinity). This is, of course, a very unfavorable property if you want to calculate an integral. If you choose a support point at exactly these divergent points, you get infinity; if you do not choose a support point at these points, you may get a value that is too low (the integral can be finite if the divergence is narrow enough).

As an example, an upper bound of error of the rectangle rule is given by[1]

$$\frac{1}{2n} sup_{0 \le x \le 1} |f'(x)| \qquad (13.4)$$

Monte Carlo Integration

Another possibility is choosing the support points randomly. This may seem very surprising at first glance, but it does have its advantages when integrating in higher dimensions.

---

[1] https://en.wikipedia.org/wiki/Numerical_integration

```
import math
import random

random.seed(0)
def f(x):
    return math.sin(x)

number_of_supporting_points = 10
I = 0
for _ in range(number_of_supporting_points):
    x = random.random()
    I += f(x)

I /= number_of_supporting_points # = 0.500
```

There are two more points to note here. Firstly, you generally have to adapt the random numbers to the range to be integrated; in this example, we integrated over the range of [0,1]. If you want to integrate over the range [0,3], you would have to transform the random numbers so that they lie in the corresponding interval. So, we need a function that maps the interval [0,1] uniformly to the interval [0,3]. This can be done by multiplying all the random numbers obtained by 3.

```
x = 3*random.random()
```

You would also have to multiply the calculated integral by the width.

```
I *= 3
```

Numerical Solution of Differential Equations

Differential Equations

As already mentioned, solving differential equations is extremely important. This is used, among other things, to calculate the aerodynamics of aircraft and the statics of buildings.

An example of solving differential equations is vibrations. A force F acts on a weight m, which is thereby pulled toward the resting point. The force is proportional to the deflection x of the weight. The differential equation that describes this system is the following:

$$m\ddot{x} = -kx \tag{13.5}$$

Or transformed:

$$\ddot{x} = -\frac{k}{m}x \tag{13.6}$$

This differential equation can be solved analytically. The solution is

$$x(t) = A \sin(\omega t + \phi) \tag{13.7}$$

where $\omega = \sqrt{\frac{k}{m}}$ is the angular frequency. The amplitude A and the phase ϕ depend on the initial conditions. However, we are not interested in the analytical solution; rather, we want to solve the differential equation numerically. To do this, we must first determine the speed of the mass and then use the speed to determine the position of the mass.

Numerical Solution of Differential Equations

$$v(t + \Delta t) = v(t) + \ddot{x}\Delta t = v(t) - \frac{k}{m}x(t) \qquad (13.8)$$

The location can be determined using the speed.

$$x(t + \Delta t) = x(t) + v(t)\Delta t \qquad (13.9)$$

If we now choose the time interval Δt small enough, we get a good approximation of the solution. We can then solve the differential equation iteratively. This is also known as the Euler method.

First, we choose the initial conditions for the location and the speed. You can also imagine it as giving the weight a push first. Let's assume the following initial conditions:

$$x(0) = 1 \qquad (13.10)$$
$$v(0) = 0 \qquad (13.11)$$
$$\frac{k}{m} = 1 \qquad (13.12)$$
$$\Delta t = 0.1 \qquad (13.13)$$

We can now calculate the first time step.

$$v(\Delta t) = v(0) - \frac{k}{m}x(0)\Delta t = 0 - 1*0.1 = -0.1 \quad x(\Delta t) = x(0) + v(0)\Delta t = 1 + 0*0.1 = 1 \quad (13.14)$$

Or rewritten in code:

```
x_0 = 1
v_0 = 0
k = 1
dt = 0.1

v = v_0 - k*x_0*dt
x = x_0 + v_0*dt
```

Now we don't just want to calculate one time step, but the entire movement. To do this, we have to repeat the calculation in a loop. We store the values of the location and the speed in a list.

```
v = [v_0]
x = [x_0]
t = [i for i in range(100)]
for _ in t:
    v.append(v[-1] - k*x[-1]*dt)
    x.append(x[-1] + v[-1]*dt)
```

We can now graphically display this movement using Matplotlib.

```
import matplotlib.pyplot as plt
plt.plot(t, x[:-1])
plt.show()
```

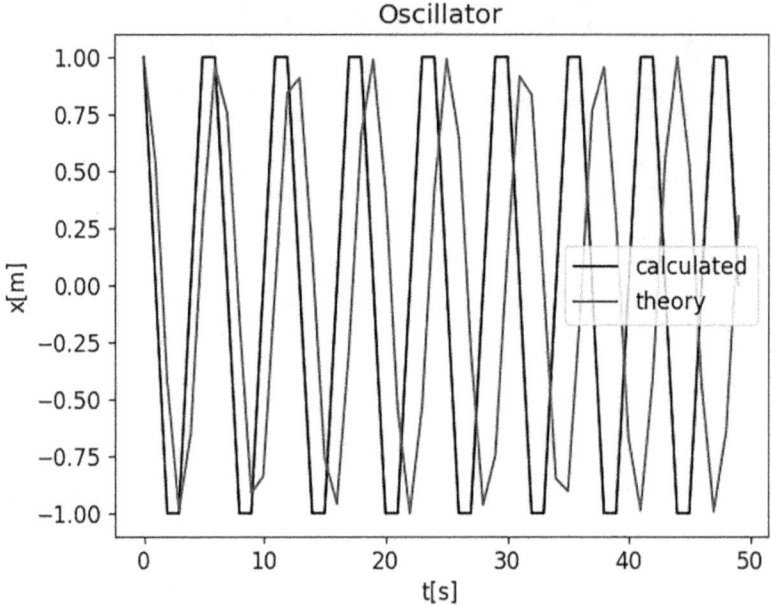

Fig. 13.5 The motion of the oscillator is calculated with numerical integration (dark gray) and the exact solution (black). The difference in the two curves occurs due to the comparably large time steps

We can now compare this solution with the analytical solution as seen in Figure 13.5. We have to make sure that the time steps are also the same.

```
x_theory = [x_0*math.cos(i/10) for i in t]

plt.plot(t, x[:-1])
plt.plot(t, x_theory)
plt.title("Oscillator")
plt.xlabel("t[s]")
plt.ylabel("x[m]")

plt.show()
```

Coupled Differential Equations

A classic example of coupled differential equations is the simulation of predators and prey. The population of these two animal species depends on the population of their own and the other animal species. If there are many prey animals, the population of predators increases; if there are few prey animals, the population of predators decreases.

This system can be described, for example, by the following differential equations: B stands for the prey animals and R for the predators.

$$\dot{B} = aB - bBR \quad \dot{R} = -cR + dBR \tag{13.15}$$

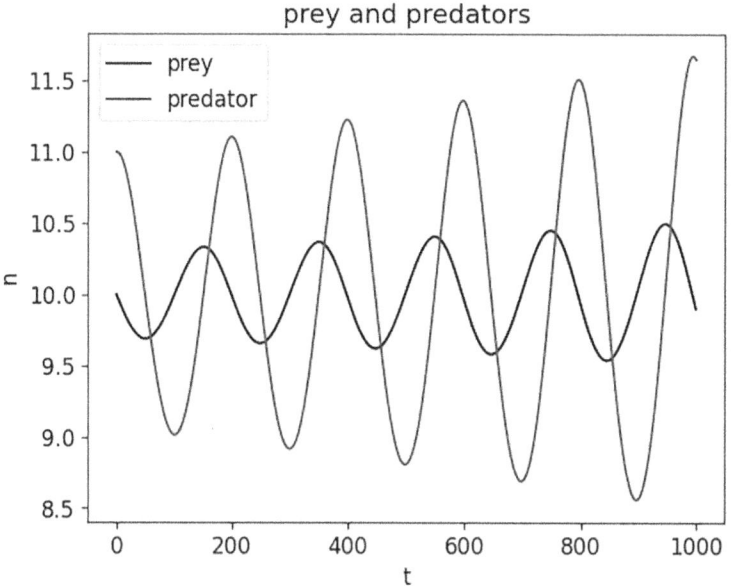

Fig. 13.6 Predator and prey population as a function of time

This system can be solved numerically, similar to the differential equations of oscillations. Analogous to the equations with x and v, we get equations for B and R. We always have to calculate one step for each size. The result of this calculation can be seen in Figure 13.6.

```
import matplotlib.pyplot as plt
import numpy as np

B = [10]
R = [11]

for i in range(1000):
    B.append(B[i] + 0.01 * B[i] - 0.001 * R[i]*B[i])
    R.append(R[i] -0.1 * R[i] + 0.01 * R[i]*B[i])

plt.plot(B)
plt.plot(R)
plt.show()
```

Some Examples

14

Percolation

Roughly speaking, percolation is the simulation of forest fires. You take a checkerboard-like pattern and randomly fill each field with a tree or desert. Then you set fire to all the trees along one side and watch how the fire spreads. If the probability exceeds a certain limit, the fire will spread to the other side. Below that limit, it will go out first.

First, we have to import a few libraries and set the random number seed.

```
from enum import Enum
import matplotlib
import matplotlib.pyplot as plt
import random

random.seed(0)
```

Now we continue with defining the types of fields. We have deserts that cannot burn, trees that can burn, and ash, i.e., trees that have already burned down. We also have burning trees that can set fire to other adjacent trees. To define these four types of fields, we use an enum. This makes the code much more readable than if we were to use "magic numbers".

```
from enum import Enum

class Field(Enum):
    DESERT = 0
    TREE = 1
    BURNING = 2
    ASH = 3
```

In the next step, we create a checkerboard-shaped field, which we initialize with trees and desert fields.

```
def initialize_map(probability_tree, size):
    map = []
    for _ in range(size):
        row = []
        for _ in range(size):
            if random.random() < probability_tree:
                row.append(Field.TREE)
            else:
```

```
            row.append(Field.DESERT)
        map.append(row)
    return map
```

An example of this map can be seen in Figure 14.1. In the next step, we define which neighbors a field has. We use periodic boundary conditions in one direction. This means that we "roll up" the chessboard from left to right. The fields of the chessboard have no neighbors at the top and bottom.

We store the coordinates of a field in a variable `Point`. This simplifies the transfer to functions because we only have to pass one variable. The x- and y-coordinates are always used together, so this definition makes sense.

```
class Point:
    def __init__(self, x, y):
        self.x = x
        self.y = y

def periodic_neighbors(point, map):
    neighbors = []
    # for illustration:
    # map = [[0, 1, 2],
    #        [3, 4, 5],
    #        [6, 7, 8]]
    # map[1][2] = 5
    length = len(map[0])
    neighbors.append(map[point.x][(point.y - 1 + length) % 1])
    neighbors.append(map[point.x][(point.y + 1) % 1])
    if point.x >= 1:
        neighbors.append(map[point.x - 1][point.y])
    if point.x <= length - 2:
        neighbors.append(map[point.x + 1][point.y])
    return neighbors
```

The code here may seem a bit confusing at first glance. To clear up the confusion, we first need to consider what the x- and y-coordinates mean in our matrix. The x-coordinate defines the row (top to bottom), and the y-coordinate defines the column (left to right) of our matrix.

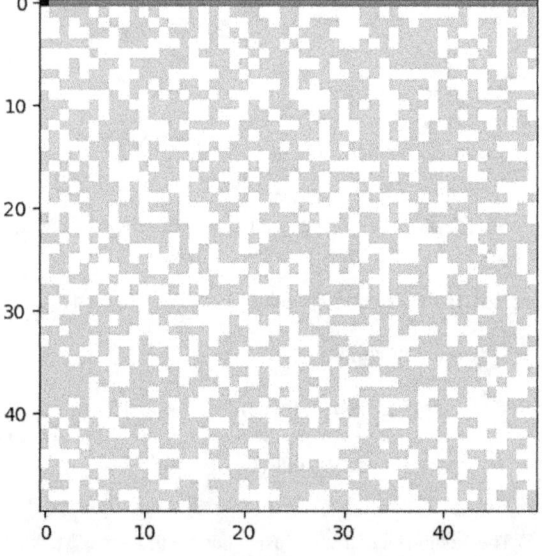

Fig. 14.1 The graphical representation of the checkerboard. The desert fields are white, the trees are light gray, the burning tries are dark gray and the burned fields are black

In the y direction, we need periodic boundary conditions. We can calculate these with the code `(dot.y - 1 + l) // l` or `(dot.y + l) // l`. This gives the value `l-1` for `y=0` and the value `0` for `y=l-1`. Calculate these values yourself. There is no better explanation than if you calculate this yourself.

In the x direction, we have no periodic boundary conditions. The matrix simply ends, and fields at the edge of the matrix only have three neighbors. So for `x=0` and `x=len(matrix)-1`, we don't need to look for neighbors in the corresponding direction. Accordingly, we have two `if` statements to check this.

Using the `periodic_neighbors` function, we can now easily determine whether a neighbor of a certain field is burning. To do this, we need to determine the neighbors and then check whether one of them is burning.

```
def neighbor_burns(point, map):
    neighbors = periodic_neighbors(point, map)
    for neighbor in neighbors:
        if neighbor == Field.BURNING:
            return True
    return False
```

The next step is to check whether a field in the matrix is starting to burn. For this to happen, it must be a tree, and a neighbor must be burning.

```
def begins_to_burn(point, map):
    if map[point.x][point.y] == Field.TREE:
        if neighbor_burns(point, map):
            return True
    return False
```

Next we have to write a function that ignites the first row of the matrix.

```
def ignite_front_row(map):
    for i in range(len(map[0])):
        map[0][i] = Field.BURNING
```

Another function that we will need is the percolation step. We take the existing matrix and check all fields to see whether they are beginning to burn. If so, we change the type of the field to `BURN`. If a field is burning, we change the type to `ASH`. Finally, we return the new matrix.

If this were a really computationally intensive application, we could certainly develop an algorithm that would be more efficient. But for our purposes here, this is good enough.

```
def percolation_step(map):
    new_map = []
    for i in range(0, len(map)):
        row = []
        for j in range(0, len(map)):
            row.append(map[i][j])
            if begins_to_burn(Point(i, j), map):
                row[-1] = Field.BURNING
            if map[i][j] == Field.BURNING:
                row[-1] = Field.ASH
        new_map.append(row)
    return new_map
```

Another important property of the matrix is whether the fire is still burning. At some point, it will go out when it can no longer ignite trees. To do this, we simply have to check whether there is still a burning field in the matrix.

```python
def still_burning(map):
    for i in range(len(map[0])):
        for j in range(len(map[0])):
            if map[i][j] == Field.BURNING:
                return True
    return False
```

As long as it is still burning, we have to carry out percolation steps. Provided we have not made any mistakes in the implementation, the fire should go out at some point.

```python
def perculate(map):
    while still_burning(map):
        map = perculation_step(map)
    return map
```

To execute the entire code, we now have to implement the following code. We will again use the already familiar `if __name__ == "__main__":` block.

```python
def main():
    map = initialize_map(0.55, 50)
    ignite_front_row(map)
    map = perculate(map)

if __name__ == "__main__":
    main()
```

The code is still a bit boring. We would like to have a graphic showing how the fire has spread. To do this, we first have to convert the fields into values.

```python
def plotable_map(map):
    m = []
    for i in range(len(map)):
        row = []
        for j in range(len(map)):
            row.append(map[i][j].value)
        m.append(row)
    return m
```

Next we define the colors we want to use for the different fields.

```python
import matplotlib

colors = ['yellow', 'green', 'red', 'black']
cmap = matplotlib.colors.ListedColormap(
        colors, name='colors', N=None)
```

Now we can display the matrix graphically. To do this, we need to import the `Matplotlib` library and display the matrix graphically after initialization and at the end of the percolation, as can be seen in Figure 14.2.

```python
def fix_color_schema(map):
    map[0][0] = Field.ASH

def main():
    map = initialize_map(0.55, 50)
    ignite_front_row(map)
    fix_color_schema(map)
    plt.imshow(plotable_map(map), cmap=cmap)
    plt.show()
    map = perculate(map)
    plt.imshow(plotable_map(map), cmap=cmap)
    plt.show()
```

Percolation

Fig. 14.2 This is the same figure as seen in Figure 14.1. The only difference is that here the forest has burned down and the fire has run out. Trees that survived the fire are shown in light gray, trees that burned down are shown in black

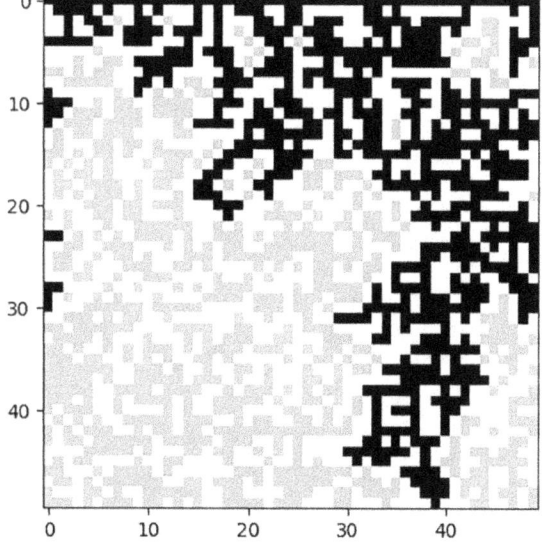

Index

A
Abstraction, 79
AI tools, 4, 28, 83, 112
append function, 21, 27
Arguments
  default, 59–60
  immutable, 13
  keyword, 58–59
  mutable, 13
Arithmetic operations, 49–50
`assert` statements, 93
Assignments, 14–15

B
`Bicycle` class, 75–76
`Bike` class, 77
`Billionaire` class, 74, 75
Boolean logic, 46
Booleans, 19–20, 30, 46, 99, 110

C
Classes
  abstraction, 79
  `Billionaire` class, 74, 75
  duck typing, 74
  example, 71–75
  global variables, 73
  inheritance (*see* Inheritance)
  vs. lists, 68
  and objects, 69–70
  `Person` class, 69, 71–74
  special methods, 70–71
  use abstract base classes, 78
Cohesion, 40–41
Comma-Separated Values (CSV) file, 85–86
Comments, 10
Components of code
  assignments, 14–15
  Booleans, 19–20
  code structure, 39
    `Car` class, 40
    cohesion, 40–41
    complexity, 40
    coupling, 40–41
    cyclic dependencies, 40
    rules, 40
  complexity, 40
  cyclic dependencies, 40
  data structures (*see* Data structures)
  dictionaries (dicts), 31–32
  enums, 34
  immutable objects, 13–14
  integers, 18–19
  lists (*see* Lists)
  mutable objects, 13–14
  none, 17
  numbers, 17, 19
    floating point numbers, 17–18
    integers, 18–19
  strings (*see* Strings)
  tuples, 32–33
  tuples *vs.* lists, 33
  types, 15
  variables, 15–16
    global, 16, 73
Control flow
  cyclic dependencies, 63
  function definition order, 62–63
  functions, 62, 63
Coupling, 40–41, 76
C programming language, 68
C++ programs, 68
CSV file, *see* Comma-Separated Values (CSV) file
Curve fitting
  covariance matrix pcov, 107
  `curve_fit` function, 107
  local minimum, 108
  and machine learning, 108
Cyclic dependencies, 40, 63

D
Data classes, 67, 68
Data structures, 20, 35
  dicts, 31
  sets, 35

trees, 64, 65
Default arguments, 59–60
Dependency injection (DI)
    faking, 101
    function objects, 98
    get_sum_of_content, 98, 99
    get_sum_of_file, 100
    MockContentProvider, 101
    mocking, 101
    polymorphic object, 99
    polymorphism, 97
    RealContentProvider, 101
    test code, 97
DI, *see* Dependency injection (DI)
__dict__ function, 70
Dictionaries (dicts), 13, 16, 31–32
Differential equations
    angular frequency, 120
    coupled differential equations, 122–123
    Euler method, 121
    vibrations, 120
Docstrings, 10
Do Not Repeat Yourself (DRY) principle, 92
Duck typing, 15, 74

E
Encapsulation, 16, 69, 78–79
Enumeration (Enums), 34
__eq__ function, 70
Euler method, 121
Exceptions, 35
    custom exceptions, 38–39
    drawbacks, 37–38
    salary, 36
    specific *vs.* general, 39
    Try/Catch/Else/Finally, 36–37
    uses, 37
ZeroDivisionError, 35

F
Files
    CSV, 85–86, 88
    HDF5, 87, 89
    JSON and Co, 86–87
    SQL, 87–88
    text file, 85
Filtering
    Apress logo, 55
    Fourier transform, 53–55
    high-pass filter, 54
    low-pass filter, 53, 54
Floating point errors, 64
For loops, 43–45, 97
Fourier transform, 53–55
Function overloading, 61–62
Functions, 57
    add function, 3, 58
    append function, 21, 27
    def keyword, 58
    factorial function, 63
    function definition order, 62–63
    function overloading, 61–62
    length, 57
    vs. methods, 57
    mutable function arguments, 13
    print function, 2, 9, 57
    random.random() function, 55
    sort function, 26

G
Gaussian bell curve, 116
Git, 2
Good code, 10, 94, 95
Google, 27, 28

H
HDF5 file, 87
Histogram, 105–106

I
IDE, *see* Integrated development environment (IDE)
If statements
    Boolean logic, 46
    Break, 47
    Continue, 47
    errors, 45
    nested, 45–46
    polymorphism, 45
    range-based for loops, 45
    Return, 47
    uses, 44–45
Images, 52–55
Immutable arguments, 13
Immutable objects, 13–14
Implementation inheritance, 75–77
Inheritance
    composition, 76
    implementation inheritance, 75–77
    interface inheritance, 77–78
    object-oriented programming, 75
__init__ function, 70, 71
__init__.py file, 81, 82
Integers, 13, 14, 17–19, 25, 64
Integrated development environment (IDE), 1, 15, 39
Interface inheritance, 75, 77–78

J
JSON file, 86–87

K
Keyword arguments, 58–60

Index

L
Labeling, 105
Libraries, 3–4, 50, 88, 125
Lists, 20
    accessing
        code, 22
        english grammar, 22
        enumerate function, 22–23
        iterator, 23
        old-school loop iterations, 23
        [] operator, 23, 24
        sublists, 24
    creation, 20–21
    list comprehension, 21–22
    merging, 27
    multidimensional, 25–26
    sorting, 26–27
    vs. strings, 25
Logical operators, 46
Loops, 43
    Break, 47
    Continue, 47
    list comprehension, 44
    lists, 44
    for loop, 43, 44
    nested, 44
    return, 47

M
Magic numbers, 59, 125
Math Module, 50, 81
Matplotlib
    basic functionality, 104
    curve fitting, 106–108
    histogram, 105–106
    labeling, 105
    plotting library, 103
    simple plot, sine function, 103
    sine curve, 103
Matrices, 25, 51–52
Modules, 81
    install packages with pip, 83
    math module, 81
    namespace package, 82–83
    packages, 81
    regular package, 81–82
    virtual environment, 84
Mountainbike class, 75–76
Mutable arguments, 13
Mutable objects, 13–14

N
Namespace package, 82–83
Naming conventions, 9
    classes, 9
    comments, 10
    docstrings, 10
    my_private_method, 10
    snake_case, 9
Naming Python, 7
    example, 7
    importance, 7
    make_appointment, 8
    names, 7, 8
    naming conventions, 9–10
    programming, 8
    readable names, 11
    rules, 9
Navier-Stokes equation, 115
Nested loop, 5, 44
None, 17
number_of_gears class, 75–76
Numbers, 17, 19
    floating point numbers, 17–18
    integers, 18–19
    magic numbers, 59
    random numbers, 55–56
    and strings, 19
Numerical integration
    estimate accuracy, 119
    Gaussian bell curve, 116
    geometric interpretation, 117–118
    higher order integration, 118–119
    integration, 116
    mathematical derivation, 116–117
    Monte Carlo integration, 119–120
Numerical mathematics
    Navier-Stokes equation, 115
    software development, 115
    three-dimensional objects, 115
NumPy, 3, 4, 25, 50, 51, 90, 109
    images, 52–53
    matrices, 51–52

P
Pandas
    bfill function, 111
    data analysis and manipulation, 109
    dropna() function, 112
    example, 109
    "Hotels" and "Booking," 110
    NaN values, 110–112
    NumPy library, 109
    price data, 113
Perculation
    checkerboard-shaped field, 125
    "magic numbers," 125
    Matplotlib library, 128
    periodic boundary conditions, 127
    periodic_neighbors function, 127
    x-and y-coordinates, 126
Person class, 69, 71–74
plt.plot() function, 103
Polymorphism, 45, 78, 97
pylint tool, 3, 39
Python
    advantages, 3

args and kwargs, 60–61
disadvantages, 3
libraries, 3–4
naming (*see* Naming Python)
REPL, 1–2
style guides
    learn programming, 4
    Software Engineering, 5
    Zen of Python, 5–6
Zen of Python, 5–6

R
Random numbers, 55
    algorithms, 55
    `gauss` function, 56
    integer numbers, 56
    Pi calculation, 56
    `random.random()` function, 55, 56
Read-Eval-Print Loop (REPL), 1–2, 26, 28
Recursion, 64
    example, 64
    `factorial` function, 63
    `get_coins` function, 64
    Trees, 64–65
Refactoring, 5, 9, 76, 91, 96
Regular package, 81–82
REPL, *see* Read-Eval-Print Loop (REPL)
`__repr__` function, 70
Roadbike class, 75–77

S
Sets, 35
Single Responsibility Principle (SRP), 41, 69
Software development, 4
    code formatting, 39
    colors, 34
    global variables, 73
    if statements (*see* If statements)
    loops (*see* Loops)
    names, 11
    naming, 7
    numerical mathematics (*see* Numerical mathematics)
    tests, 91
Software engineer, coding activities, 8
Software Engineering, 5, 6, 69
`sort` function, 26–27
SQL, *see* Structured Query Language (SQL)
SRP, *see* Single Responsibility Principle (SRP)
`__str__` function, 70, 71
Strings, 19, 28
    contains function, 30
    f-strings, 29
    vs. lists, 25
    and numbers, 19
    operations, 30
    property, 28
    quotation marks/closing marks, 28, 29
    special characters, 29
    syntax, 28
    types, 29
    uses, 29
`str` notation, 67
Structured Query Language (SQL), 87–88
    database technology, 87
    MySQL, 88
    PostgreSQL, 88
    SQLite, 88

T
TDD, *see* Test-Driven Development (TDD)
Test code, 94
Test-Driven Development (TDD)
    Fizz Buzz game, 95–97
    production code, 95
    steps, 95
Tests, 91
`test_square.py` file, 92, 93
Time
    decorators, 90
    performance, 90
    `time` module, 89
    timing functions, 89–90
Trees, 64–65, 125–127, 129
Tuples, 32
    divmod function, 32
    function, 33
    vs. lists, 33
    [] operator, 32
    syntax, 32
    unpacking, 32–33

U
Unit tests, 92–94

V
Variables, 15, 46
    code, 16
    global variables, 16, 73
    properties, 15
    values, 16
Virtual environments, 4, 84, 94

W
Writing tests, 91

GPSR Compliance
The European Union's (EU) General Product Safety Regulation (GPSR) is a set of rules that requires consumer products to be safe and our obligations to ensure this.

If you have any concerns about our products, you can contact us on

ProductSafety@springernature.com

In case Publisher is established outside the EU, the EU authorized representative is:

Springer Nature Customer Service Center GmbH
Europaplatz 3
69115 Heidelberg, Germany

www.ingramcontent.com/pod-product-compliance
Lightning Source LLC
LaVergne TN
LVHW081450060526
838201LV00050BA/1760